IMAGES
of America

SOMERSET
COUNTY
CROSSROADS OF THE
AMERICAN REVOLUTION

In 1776, George Washington was only 44 years old, not the elder statesman portrayed on the dollar bill. He spent more time in central New Jersey, especially Somerset County, than in any other place during the American Revolution. (David Memorial Library.)

IMAGES
of America

SOMERSET
COUNTY
CROSSROADS OF THE
AMERICAN REVOLUTION

William A. Schleicher
and Susan J. Winter

ARCADIA
PUBLISHING

Published by Arcadia Publishing
Charleston, South Carolina

Library of Congress Catalog Card Number: 99-61281

For all general information contact Arcadia Publishing at:
Telephone 843-853-2070
Fax 843-853-0044
E-mail sales@arcadiapublishing.com
For customer service and orders:
Toll-Free 1-888-313-2665

Visit us on the Internet at www.arcadiapublishing.com

CONTENTS

ACKNOWLEDGMENTS

To the many people who have shared their treasured photographs and stories with us, we extend our heartfelt thanks: John Albright, Thomas D'Amico, Bill Amerman, George Bebbington, Ernest Bowers, Wayne Daniels, William Brahms, Mike Deak, Susan Feibush, James S. Jones, Davis Gray, Jessie Havens, H. (Hap) Heins, George Hunter, June Kennedy, James Kurzenberger, Wesley Ott, Herbert Patullo, Charles Stone, Dorothy Stratford, Harry Kels Swan, and Douglas Winterich.

We would also like to thank the following organizations for giving us access to their archives: Bernards Township Library, Biblioteque National of Paris, Branchburg Historic Preservation Commission, Branchburg Historical Society, Brigade of the American Revolution, Clarence Dillon Memorial Library, Connecticut Historical Society, David Memorial Library, Franklin Township Library, Independence National Historic Park, the Library of Congress, Morristown National Historic Park, the Museum of the City of New York, Neshanic Station Historical Society, the New Jersey State Park System, New York Historical Society, Old Barracks Museum, Peapack Gladstone Cultural and Heritage Commission, Rutgers University Special New Jersey Collection, Somerset County Historical Society, Somerset County Library, Somerset County Planning Board, *Somerset Messenger Gazette*, Swan Historical Foundation, and the Wallace House Collection.

Please note that the names in parentheses at the end of each caption indicate the source of the image, not the source of the information for the caption. All images credited to the Swan Historical Foundation, of which Harry Kels Swan is the president, are on display (along with many other items) at the Visitors Center, Washington's Crossing State Park.

The cover photograph, by Frank Cecala, was provided by the Brigade of the American Revolution, Inc., an international nonprofit organization whose members recreate the life and times of the common people of the American War for Independence. For information, visit the organization's website at www.brigade.org or call toll free 1-(800)-GoRevWar.

INTRODUCTION

Located halfway between New York and Philadelphia, astride two of the major routes connecting those cities, it is little wonder that Somerset County, NJ, was destined to become the "Crossroads of the Revolution." Armies of Great Britain, France, and the United States crossed and recrossed the county from east to west and from north to south.

When the Provincial Congress of New Jersey passed an act in 1775 that required each county to form a militia, it noted with approval that Somerset County already had one. The president of the Provincial Congress of New Jersey, Hendrick Fisher, and the first and second secretaries, William Patterson and Frederick Frelinghuysen, were all from Somerset County. Of New Jersey's 21 counties, only Somerset can boast two of the state's five signers of the Declaration of Independence, Richard Stockton and John Witherspoon. A third, John Hart, was from Pennington, located in Hunterdon County.

The first governor of the state of New Jersey, William Livingston, lived in Basking Ridge during the time the British occupied Elizabethtown. His friend and fellow parishioner, Elias Boudinot, also sought refuge there. Boudinot was elected president of the Continental Congress in 1782 and 1783, and it was he who signed the treaty of peace that ended the war. During the Revolution, the man who was to become New Jersey's second governor, William Patterson, lived on a plantation that had been confiscated from a loyalist in the Bradley Gardens section of Bridgewater.

General Washington spent more time in Somerset County than anywhere else during the Revolutionary War. Two of the headquarters in which he spent months, the Wallace House in Somerville, and Rockingham in Rocky Hill, are maintained as parks, and are open to the public. Martha Washington lived with him in both of these residences. The most famous generals on both sides and their military units spent time in Somerset County. These generals included William Alexander Lord Stirling, Benedict Arnold, Philemon Dickinson, Nathaniel Greene, Henry Knox, Charles Lee, Benjamin Lincoln, Daniel Morgan, Israel Putnam, Arthur St. Clair, Baron von Steuben, John Sullivan, and Anthony Wayne. French generals included the Count de Custine, the Marquis de Lafayette, the Duke de Lauzun, Chevalier Du Portail, and the Count de Rochambeau. Among the British generals were Sir William Howe, Sir Henry Clinton, and Charles Lord Cornwallis. Alexander Hamilton, Aaron Burr, and Lighthorse Harry Lee were majors. There were state visits from the French ambassador, the Spanish envoy, and chiefs from the Delaware Indian Nation. Thomas Jefferson and James Monroe came here to visit the Washingtons.

It was here that the American soldiers spent their coldest winter. Here, the first military academy was established, General von Steuben wrote his *Regulations for the Infantry of the*

United States, Washington planned the Iroquois Campaign, and the 13-star flag was first flown over American troops following its adoption by Congress. Other important events that took place in Somerset County include the capture by the British of Major General Charles Lee, the Battle of Bound Brook, and many lesser skirmishes. The most important battle was the one that didn't happen—by refusing to fight the British on the fields of Franklin and Hillsborough, Washington forced Howe to change his strategy, lose several months time, and ultimately, lose the war in the North.

Following the war, historians from the big cities wrote of its effects on Boston, New York, and Philadelphia. The Revolution, however, was fought in New Jersey more than anywhere else. Somerset County has more Revolutionary War history than the entire state of Connecticut. Yet there they worship history while here we sacrifice it to "progress." As you read this book, you may grieve over how much has been lost, but you will also be amazed by what still remains. It is the authors' hope that you will be motivated to let your elected officials and planning boards know how important it is to preserve what remains of our state's historical sites and buildings.

We are indebted to Ernest Bowers for the following (partial) list of American and French military units that served in Somerset County between 1776 and 1783. British and Hessian forces stationed in New Brunswick in the Spring of 1777 are enumerated on p. 62.

American Forces:

Hazen's 2nd Canadian Regiment
Butler's Connecticut Detachment
4th and 8th Connecticut Regiments
1st Delaware Regiment
Independents
Grayson's Regiment
Hartley's Additional Regiment
Georgia Troops
Maine Troops
1st through 7th Maryland Regiments
German Battalion (8th Maryland)
9th through 14th Massachusetts Regiments
1st through 3rd New Hampshire Regiments
1st through 4th New Jersey Regiments
2nd and 4th New York Regiments
Patton's Additional Regiment
3rd North Carolina Regiment
1st through 13th Pennsylvania Regiments
1st and 2nd Rhode Island Regiments
Sherburne's Additional Regiment
Spencer's Additional Regiment
1st through 16th Virginia Regiments
1st and 2nd Virginia State Regiments
Washington's Life Guard
Morgan's Ranger Corps

Armand's Legion (Ottendorf's Corps)
Baldwin's Quartermaster Artificers
Rowe's Company of Artillery Artificers
1st through 3rd Battalions of Artillery
Somerset County Militia
Hunterdon County Militia
Wyoming PA (Connecticut) Militia
von Heer's Provost Corps
1st through 4th Regiments of Light Dragoons
Jackson's Regiment
W. Lee's Regiment
3rd, 14th, 19th, 23rd, and 26th Continental Inf.

French Forces:

13th Rgt. Bourbonnais Infanterie
26th Rgt. Portore Infanterie (one company)
41st Rgt. Soissonois Infanterie
64th Rgt. Auxonne Artillerie
68th Rgt. de Beauce Infanterie (one company)
70th Rgt. Medoc Infanterie (one company)
84th Rgt. de Rohan-Soribise Infanterie
85th Rgt. Saintonage Infanterie
104th Rgt. Royal Deux Ponts Infanterie
Lauzun's Legion of Foreign Volunteers

One

THE FOMENT OF WAR

As the people strain under the "Intolerable Acts," the Dutch clergy preach liberty from the pulpit. There are dark days as Washington retreats across New Jersey after his defeat on Long Island. Minute men and loyalists clash in Branchburg, and General Charles Lee is captured by the British in Basking Ridge.

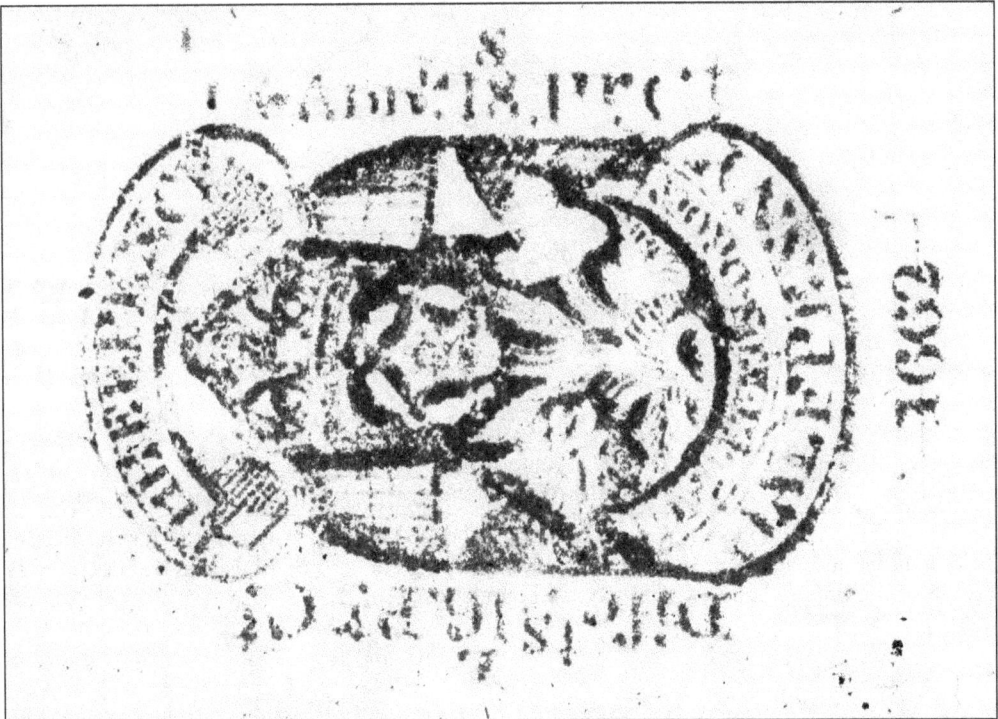

Britain passed a number of measures designed to tax the colonies and put restrictions on trade. Collectively, they were known as the "Intolerable Acts." One of these laws was the Stamp Act, which put a tax on every document written or passed in the colonies. The rallying cry of the Revolution became "No taxation without representation!" This half-penny tax stamp is from a newspaper of the period. The half-penny tax was included in the 6 1/2¢ price of the paper. (Author's Collection.)

On September 17, 1765, New York merchant Theodore Van Wyck sent this letter to Michael Field, a miller and merchant in Bound Brook, expressing concern that business had declined as a result of the Stamp Act. (Swan Historical Foundation.)

Perth Amboy August 25. 1772

Sir,

       I have it in Command from His Excellency the Governor to inform you that a Battalion of His Majesty's Troops is daily expected to arrive in this Province, and to require you immediately to put the Barracks under your Care into proper Condition for the Reception of such Parts of the said Battalion as may be ordered into them for Quarters

              I am, Sir
                Your most obedient
                  Servant
                  Cha. Pettit

Hendrick Fisher Esqr

This letter from Charles Pettit, dated August 25, 1772, is addressed to Hendrick Fisher, the barrack master at New Brunswick. Fisher was being ordered to make the barracks ready to receive a contingent of royal troops. (Rutgers Special New Jersey Collection.)

Hendrick Fisher lived in this house on his 1,700-acre plantation in Franklin Township. Today, the house is located on Easton Avenue and belongs to the Ukrainian Orthodox Church. It has been opened to the public for special occasions. (Frederick N. Voorhees photo, Somerset County Historical Society.)

Hendrick Fisher was a firebrand of the American Revolution. He was the head of the Committee of Correspondence, and elected the first president of the Provincial Congress of New Jersey. He stood in front of Harpending House (see p. 59) and read the Declaration of Independence aloud to the citizens of Bound Brook just days after it was signed in Philadelphia. The event is commemorated each Fourth of July by the Camp Middlebrook Association. (Frederick N. Voorhees photo, Somerset County Historical Society.)

Hendrick Fisher did not survive to see his dream of independence realized. He died in 1779 at the age of 82. His grave may be seen in the Fisher family cemetery, which is now part of the Ukranian Orthodox cemetery on Easton Avenue, in Franklin Township. (Frederick N. Voorhees photo, Somerset County Historical Society.)

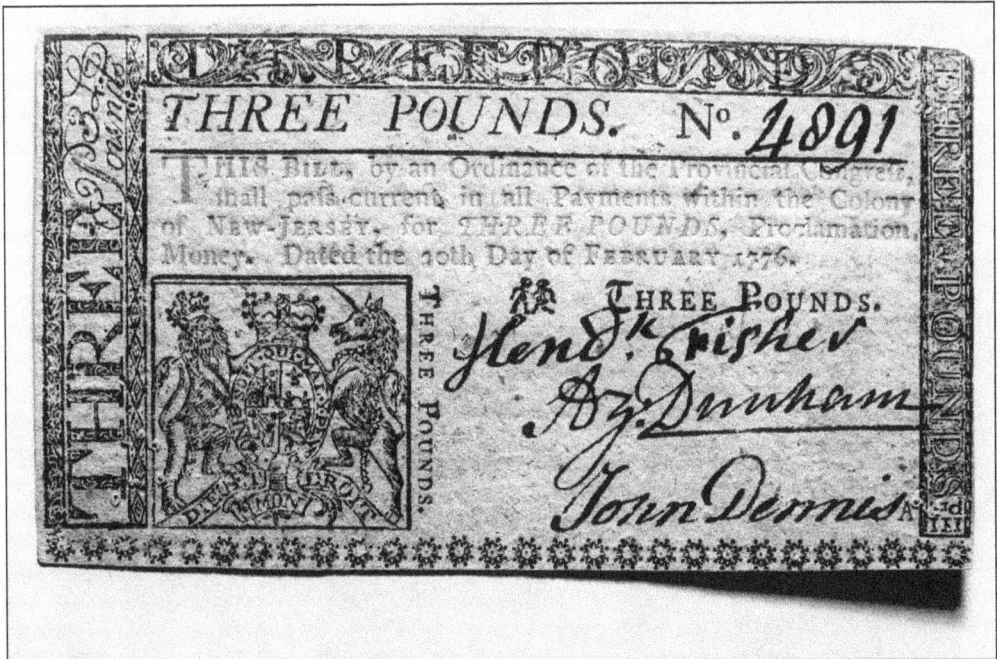

During the American Revolution, the Provincial Congress of New Jersey issued its own currency. This £3 note, issued February 20, 1776, was signed by President Hendrick Fisher. The other two signers were also from Somerset County. (Swan Historical Foundation.)

The British put a price on Hendrick Fisher's head. When they offered a general amnesty to any who would swear allegiance to the crown, Hendrick Fisher and a handful of others were specifically excluded. This note in Peter Dumont's journal shows that, at times, Fisher hid out in South Branch, living with the Dumont family and working in their mill and general store. Peter Dumont was a fierce supporter of the patriot cause. His son, John Baptist Dumont, was known locally as John Protest Dumont for his role on the Committee of Safety and the formation of the militia. (Rutgers Special New Jersey Collection.)

The miller's house in South Branch, Hillsborough Township, still stands beside the river. It later became the home of Peter Dumont Vroom, who was elected governor of New Jersey in 1829. (Branchburg Historical Society.)

Also located in Hillsborough, the pre-Revolutionary Voorhees homestead is at Blackwell's Mills. (Rutgers Special New Jersey Collection.)

The Abraham Du Bois House, pictured here *c.* 1890, was constructed *c.* 1757 on the site of an older structure. Abraham Du Bois was a member of the Hillsborough Committee of Safety in 1776 and 1777. (Historic American Buildings Survey, New Jersey #334, Library of Congress.)

William Patterson (left), a lawyer from Raritan, was elected secretary, and Frederick Frelinghuysen (right) was elected assistant secretary of the Provincial Congress of New Jersey, under Hendrick Fisher. Patterson bought an estate confiscated from loyalist Barnardus LaGrange, in what is now Bradley Gardens. Patterson later became the first attorney general of the state of New Jersey, and its second governor. (Wallace House Collection.)

The Frelinghuysen House is presently the public library in Raritan. The wooden wing dates from the time of the Revolution. The brick part was added by Frederick Frelinghuysen after the war. This is a view of the front of the old part of the house, which faces away from the road. (Historic American Buildings Survey, New Jersey #332, Library of Congress.)

16

Frederick Frelinghuysen was a colonel in the 1st Battalion of the Somerset County Militia. He was credited with firing the shot that killed Colonel Johann Rall, the commander of the Hessian forces in the Battle of Trenton on December 26, 1776. Frelinghuysen later became a major general during the Whiskey Rebellion. (Historic American Buildings Survey, New Jersey #332, Library of Congress.)

Kept as a tavern from 1730 to 1756 by George Middagh, this house is the oldest in the borough of Raritan. Early town meetings were held here. (Historic American Buildings Survey, New Jersey #333, Library of Congress.)

Because this company of the 2nd Battalion of Somerset County Militia (minutemen) met at the Neshanic Dutch Reformed Church, they were called the "Shanick Company." Their first captain, John Ten Eyck, was killed in a skirmish with the British at Somerset Court House (Millstone) June 17, 1777. (Drawing by John Albright, Courtesy Neshanic Depot, Charles Stone Collection.)

The Neshanic Dutch Reformed Church began to meet in 1752. The building, erected from Sourland Mountain stone in 1759, is the oldest church building in the county. Most of the population of Somerset County was of Dutch descent. Dutch was spoken in daily life and in the churches until well into the 1800s. The Dutch tended to be strongly patriotic, and made Somerset County a safe haven for Washington and his troops. (Neshanic Station Historical Society.)

Reverends Jacob Rutsen Hardenbergh (left) and John Peter Gabriel Muhlenberg (right) preached liberty from the pulpit. Muhlenberg was the minister in the Lutheran church in Pluckemin until just before the war. In Virginia, in 1775, he preached "that there was a time to fight, and that time had now come." Removing his vestments to reveal his colonel's uniform, he enlisted most of his congregation that day. Muhlenburg returned to Somerset County in the service of his country. (Rutgers Special New Jersey Collection.)

The old Dutch Parsonage was built with bricks from Holland that were given as a wedding gift from the parents of Dinah Van Burgh, upon her marriage to Reverend John Frelinghuysen. Dinah and John were the parents of Colonel Frederick Frelinghuysen (see pp. 16 and 17). After John died, Dinah married the Reverend Jacob Hardenbergh. Hardenbergh was the first president of Queens College (Rutgers) and was a neighbor and advisor to General Washington during the second Middlebrook encampment. This house is still open to the public. (Historic American Buildings Survey, New Jersey #294, Library of Congress.)

This plea for flour to feed 3,000 hungry men was written by Robert Ogden, commissary for the Flying Camp, to Michael Field, a miller from Bound Brook, on July 30, 1776. The Flying Camp consisted of militia from New Jersey, Maryland, and Pennsylvania. It was formed during the summer of 1776 to protect New Jersey from invasion by the British through Staten Island. (Swan Historical Foundation.)

Great Britain sent its best generals and fighting units in an attempt to put a quick end to the rebellion and set an example for the rest of the Empire. In August 1776, General Washington was defeated on Long Island by a vastly superior army of British and Hessian soldiers. The rest of 1776 consisted of the beleaguered and dwindling American army falling back across New Jersey and crossing Somerset County by various routes. This picture shows the British troops looting the New Jersey homes of patriots and loyalists alike as they pursued the American troops. These actions served to turn the population of the area against the British. (Connecticut Historical Society.)

Loyalist lawyer Barnardus LaGrange lived in this stone house (pictured here in 1868) at the corner of Albany and Neilson Streets in a section of New Brunswick that was then part of Somerset County. LaGrange had fled the wrath of his neighbors when Washington occupied the vacant house from November 29 to December 1, 1776. From here, Washington wrote a letter ordering the procurement of a fleet of boats to move the army across the Delaware River. Later, after the Battle of Monmouth, General Charles Lee was imprisoned here during his court-martial, and still later, British Colonel John Simcoe was secretly held prisoner here to protect him from lynch mobs. (Rutgers Special New Jersey Collection.)

The home of Abraham Ten Eyck is on a hill along Old York Road, overlooking the confluence of the Raritan River in Branchburg. His 500-acre estate extended from the Raritan River to the Hunterdon County line. Abraham Ten Eyck was colonel of the 1st Battalion of the Somerset County Militia. In early 1776, Colonel Ten Eyck was ordered by the Provincial Congress of New Jersey to apprehend a long list of loyalists in Hunterdon County and bring them before the Committee of Safety. (Branchburg Historical Society.)

On December 8, 1776, there was a skirmish at the confluence of the Raritan River, when 200 mounted loyalists attempted to cross the river to join the British against General Washington. The minutemen had been alerted as the horsemen passed through Readington Village and were waiting at the river in ambush. After a sharp fight, the loyalists were driven up North Branch River Road, where a second fight ensued as they met the North Branch militia company answering the call. (*The Somerset Messenger Gazette.*)

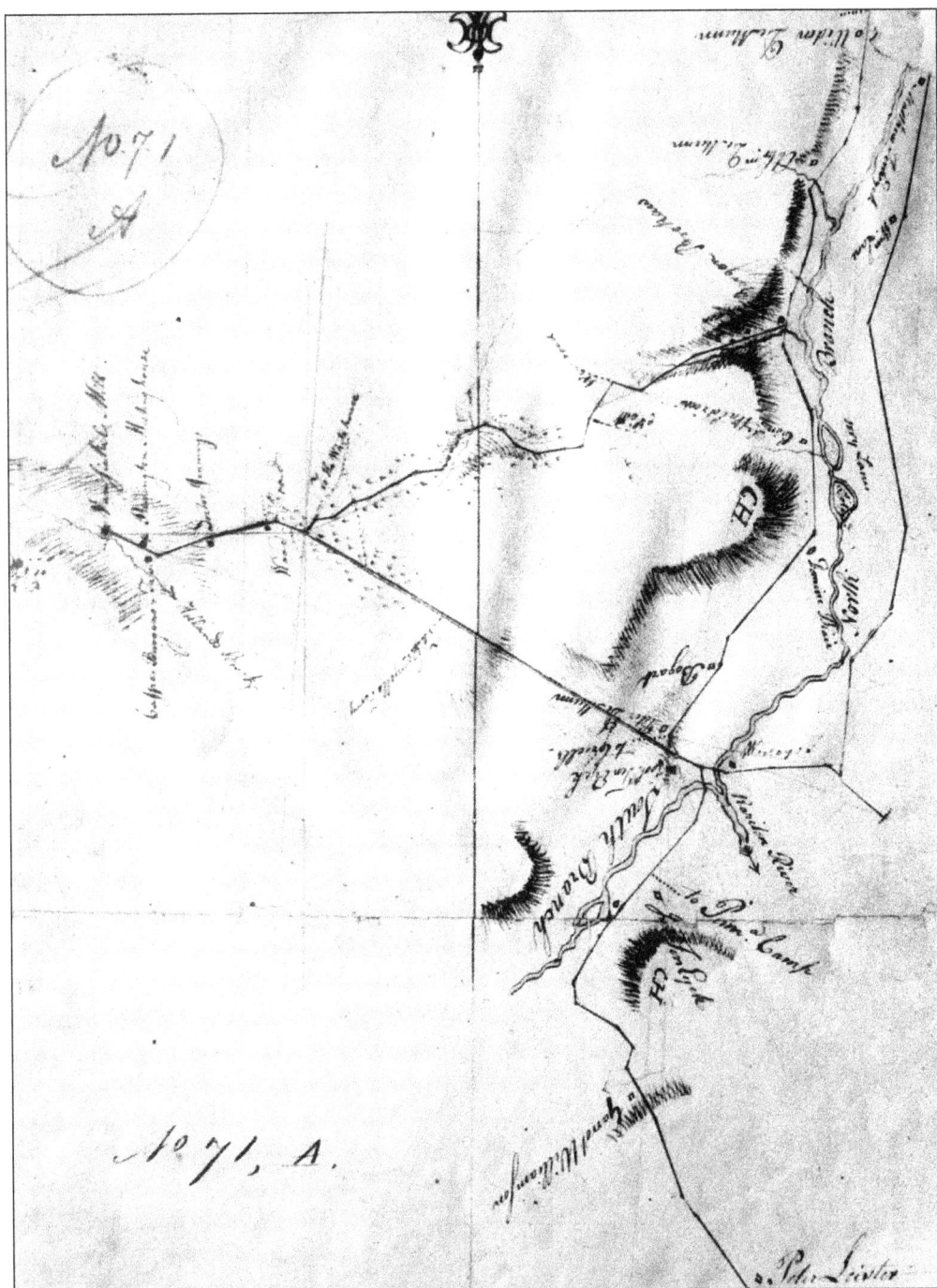

Robert Erskine, surveyor general for Washington, made maps of Somerset County during the Middlebrook encampment. This map shows part of Branchburg. The confluence of the Raritan River is seen just below the midpoint of the map on the right, and Readington Village is seen just above the midpoint on the left. The straight line between them is Old York Road. Note that there was a second bridge at the confluence, leading to Hillsborough, giving the area the name Two Bridges. (New York Historical Society.)

The DEPUTIES *of the several Counties of* New-Jersey *in* PROVINCIAL CONGRESS.

To Jacob Ten Eyck Esqr.

WE reposing especial Trust and Confidence in your Patriotism, Valour, Conduct and Fidelity, Do, by Virtue of the Power and Authority delegated to us by our Constituents, and in Pursuance of the Direction of the Honourable the Continental Congress, constitute and appoint you the said Jacob Ten Eyck Captain of a Company in the first Regiment of Foot Militia in the County of Somerset, where of the Right Honorable William Earl of Stirling is Colonel, during the Will & pleasure of the provincial Congress. You are therefore to take the said Company into your Charge and Care as Captain thereof, and duly to exercise both Officers and Soldiers of that Company in Arms. And as they are hereby directed to obey you as their Captain so you are likewise to observe and follow such Orders and Directions from Time to Time as you shall receive from your superior Officer or Officers, The Provincial Congress or Committee of Safety: And for your so doing this shall be your Commission. Dated the Thirtieth day of August 1775.

By Order of the Congress,

Attested

Fredk. Frelinghuysen Dep. Secy.   Hendk. Fisher, Presidt.

Jacob Ten Eyck from North Branch was given a commission as a captain of militia by the Provincial Congress of New Jersey. This is a copy of his commission, signed by President Hendrick Fisher and Deputy Secretary Frederick Frelinghuysen, both from Somerset County. (Rutgers Special New Jersey Collection.)

In 1700, Mathias Ten Eyck bought 500 acres of land from John Johnstone. In 1720, he deeded the land to his son Jacob, who built a one-and-one-half story house on the property. Jacob served in the French and Indian War. His son Jacob was captain of the North Branch Militia (see above). After the war, Jacob Jr. added the second story of this house, making it the way it looks today. (Branchburg Historical Society.)

24

To Capt Jacob Ten Eyck.

You are Desired to Distribute of the Powder in your Custody in the following manner — to Capt Hall at his Request 8th weight of Said Powder and also to Capt Roelof Sebring 5 Pounds and to the Bound Brook Company when their Captain Shall be Established 8 P[oun]d and Preserve to your Self 7 Pounds weight and Take their Receipt for the Same —

May 21st 1776 } By order of the Committee

Edward Bunn Chairman

Because of his relatively secure location, Jacob Ten Eyck of North Branch was assigned to stockpile and guard gunpowder for the militia. This document orders him to issue varying amounts of gunpowder to different militia captains. (Rutgers Special New Jersey Collection.)

This pre-Revolutionary house is the oldest in the village of North Branch. When it was built in the mid-1700s, people lived in one part of the house and the farm animals lived in the other. (Branchburg Historic Preservation Commission.)

The small wing on the right side of this Branchburg home is the original pre-Revolutionary house, built c. 1750. At that time, there was outside cellar access, and cows were kept in the cellar. The larger wing was constructed in 1837. (George Hunter Collection.)

This one-and-a-half-story, pre-Revolutionary house is located on Old York Road in Branchburg. (Branchburg Historic Preservation Commission.)

This Branchburg house was the home of Guisbert Bogert during the Revolution. Bogert owned a slave named Samuel. Casper Berger, from Readington Village, asked Samuel to serve in the militia in his place. Samuel agreed, so Casper bought him from Guisbert Bogert. Samuel fought in the Battles of Long Island, Two Bridges, Princeton, Van Nest's Mill, Monmouth, and in the Sullivan Campaign against the Iroquois in upstate New York. (Branchburg Historical Society)

In 1776, Major Gen. Charles Lee (left) resigned a British lieutenant colonelcy to become second in command to General Washington; this act caused him to be despised in England. English Coronet Banastre Tarleton (right) vowed to "cut off the head of that turncoat, Charles Lee!" After the war, it was said around London that "Tarleton boasts of having butchered more men and lain with more women than anybody else in the army." To this statement someone replied, "Lain with! What a weak expression! He should have said ravished. Rapes are the relaxation of murderers!" (David Memorial Library.)

As Washington was being pushed back across New Jersey, he repeatedly sought reinforcements from General Lee. Lee was jealous of Washington and thought that he himself would make a better commander-in-chief. Lee's army belatedly reached Bedminster by the evening of December 12, 1776, and Lee decided to spend the night with the lovely widow White at her tavern (seen here) in Basking Ridge, some 5 miles away. (Somerset County Historical Society.)

British Lieutenant Colonel William Harcourt took 25 men from the 16th Regiment of Light Dragoons, who were stationed at Pennington on a scouting party, to locate Lee's army. Among Harcourt's hand-picked officers was Coronet Tarleton, who was assigned as advanced guard with five men. Pushing north on the road to Morristown, Tarleton captured an express rider with a letter from General Lee to General Sullivan, his second in command, with the army at Pluckemin. Learning of General Lee's whereabouts, Tarleton and his men rushed the widow White's tavern, making as much noise as possible. The sentries panicked, dropped their arms, and fled. Lee's aide-de-camp, two French colonels, and some of the guard kept firing from the tavern for about eight minutes. Tarleton ordered Lee to surrender, or else the tavern would be burned and everyone would be put to the sword. General Lee surrendered to Lieutenant Colonel Harcourt, and was quickly tied on a spare horse in his shirt and blanket coat with no hat. A slave at the tavern reported that the general's queue was cut off as a souvenir. The dragoons hustled their prisoner south, through Hillsborough, to General Lord Cornwallis at Pennington. Lee remained a prisoner of the British until 1778. General Sullivan assumed command of Lee's army, marching west on Lamington Road to New Germantown (Oldwick), and then south to join Washington in Pennsylvania. (*Scribner's History of the United States*, 1879.)

In 1766, this stone house was built by William Annin, off Lyons Road in Bernards Township. During the Revolution, it served as a church, school, and hospital. Annin later served in the New Jersey State Legislature. (Bernards Township Library.)

A date stone at the peak of the east gable indicates that this house was built in 1764, perhaps by John Van Compen. The house stands near the corner of Valley Road and Stone House Road in Bernards Township, a section of town named "Stone House," after this house. (Historic American Buildings Survey New Jersey #247, Library of Congress.)

Two

IN THE YEAR 1777

Following the Battles of Trenton and Princeton, Washington's triumphant army receives warm welcomes at Millstone and Pluckemin. The first Middlebrook encampment is Washington's response to the sacking and burning of mills and farms in Somerset County. British generals launch an attack on Bound Brook, and taunt Washington to fight on the plains of Franklin.

After a humiliating defeat on Long Island, having been forced to retreat across New Jersey, Washington turned the tide of the war with three smashing victories—the Battle of Trenton; the Battle of the Second Assunpink; and the Battle of Princeton. Following the victory at Princeton on January 3, 1777, Washington wanted to march on to New Brunswick and take the British stores, but his men were weary from days of marching and fighting with no sleep and little, if any, food. At this spot in the Presbyterian cemetery in Kingston, Washington held a conference on horseback with his generals. He decided to turn his victorious but exhausted army north through Somerset County and establish winter quarters. (William Brahms.)

Word was sent ahead that Washington's victorious army was approaching, and that the men needed to be fed. The citizens of Hillsborough prepared food and met the army when it arrived in Millstone at dusk on January 3, 1777. General Washington and some of his staff were quartered in the home of John Van Doren, which may still be seen just south of the village of Millstone. This scene was photographed in 1937. (Historic American Buildings Survey, New Jersey #293, Library of Congress.)

This is another view of the Van Doren House. Some months later, in 1777, British soldiers looted the house. Mrs. Van Doren refused to give them her keys or tell them where the family valuables were hidden. The soldiers hung her by her feet in the cellar and ransacked the house. She was "almost dead" by the time she was rescued by her neighbors. This photograph was taken about 1900. (Somerset County Historical Society.)

Following the Battle of Princeton, Washington and his staff were riding across the battlefield when they saw some British soldiers ministering to a fallen officer. Upon learning who it was, Washington's physician, Dr. Benjamin Rush (left), asked to be permitted to attend him. Rush had lived at the home of the wounded officer's parents while attending medical school in Scotland. Captain William Leslie was placed in a wagon along with wounded Americans but died on the way from Millstone to Pluckemin. His grave (right) may be seen in the Pluckemin Presbyterian Church cemetery. (Edythe Van Doren Collection.)

Built *c.* 1750, the Matthew Lane House served as Washington's headquarters while in Pluckemin, following the Battle of Princeton. Dr. Benjamin Rush and Generals Greene, Knox, and Sullivan were also quartered here. General and Mrs. Washington stayed here for two nights in February 1779, during the grand ball celebrating the first anniversary of the French alliance (see p. 97). The house was destroyed in the 1940s by the Pluckemin Presbyterian Church to make way for a parking lot. (Edythe Van Doren Collection.)

The small wing on the left side of this house was the original Jacob Eoff Tavern, built in 1750. The Committee of Safety met here. Continental army and militia officers mingled here January 4–6, 1777, following the Battle of Princeton. During the second Middlebrook encampment, December 1778–May 1779, some of General Knox's officers were quartered here. The building burned down in 1980. (James S. Jones Collection.)

The William McEowen House is believed to be the first house erected in the village of Pluckemin. At the time of the Revolution, a store was kept here. Squire McEowen was a commissary for the American army. A British foraging party ransacked the store and carried off all of its boots, shoes, and clothing, among other things. (Somerset County Historical Society.)

This old stone house, made famous by Andrew Mellick's *Story of an Old Farm*, was built by Johannes David Moelich in 1751. General Sullivan was quartered in this house on the night that General Charles Lee stayed at the Widow White's tavern. Members of the Mellick family recalled years later the commotion that ensued when word of Lee's capture reached General Sullivan (see p. 29). (Rutgers Library Special New Jersey Collection.)

The Gaston House, on Lamington Road in Pluckemin, is still standing. During the Revolutionary War, Robert Gaston was a private, and Joseph Gaston was paymaster. (Edythe Van Doren Collection.)

Linnfields was built in the mid-1700s by Alexander Linn, a judge of the Court of Common Pleas who served as a major in the 1st Brigade of the Somerset County Militia during the Revolution. His son James sought a life in politics after graduating from Princeton. He was elected to the New Jersey State Senate and, in 1799, to the Congress. When the presidential election was thrown into the House of Representatives, Linn cast the deciding vote for Thomas Jefferson over Aaron Burr. (Author's Collection.)

This house was built in 1765 by Scottish immigrants David and Mary Kirkpatrick. David served as a private in the 1st Brigade, Somerset County Militia, and was wounded in June 1780. (Author's Collection.)

36

Elias Boudinot and his wife, Hannah Stockton Boudinot, found themselves to be refugees when the British occupied their hometown of Elizabethtown in the spring of 1777. Boudinot later became the president of the Continental Congress, a position roughly equivalent to president of the United States. He was one of the signers of the Treaty of Paris, which ended the war. (Independence National Historic Park.)

This house, located just north of the town of Basking Ridge, was purchased by Hannah and Elias Boudinot in 1771 to provide them with a refuge from the impending hostilities. After the war, in 1787, Samuel Lewis Southard was born here. He became a U.S. senator, secretary of the Navy, governor of New Jersey, president of the Senate, and acting vice president of the United States under President Tyler. (Somerset County Planning Board.)

Shown here are William Alexander, Lord Earl Stirling (left), and William Livingston (right), the governor of New Jersey and the brother of Mrs. Stirling. Governor Livingston became a house guest of the Stirlings early in 1777, when the British occupied Elizabethtown. Many refugees came to northern Somerset County. General Zebulon Pike was born in Lamington, where his parents were refugees. (Rutgers Library Special New Jersey Collection.)

I *William Alexander Earl of Stirling major General in the armies of the United States* do acknowledge the UNITED STATES of AME-RICA, to be Free, Independent and Sovereign States, and declare that the people thereof owe no allegiance or obedience to George the Third, King of Great-Britain; and I renounce, refuse and abjure any allegiance or obedience to him; and I do *Swear* that I will to the utmost of my power, fupport, maintain and defend the faid United States, againft the faid King George the Third, his heirs and fucceffors and his or their abettors, affiftants and adherents, and will ferve the faid United States in the office of *Major General* — which I now hold, with fidelity, according to the beft of my fkill and underftanding.

Sworn before at the Camp at Valley forge the 12th May 1778 *Stirling,* *G. Washington*

This is the oath of allegiance signed by Major General William Alexander and Lord Stirling, and witnessed by George Washington, at Valley Forge on May 12, 1776. (*Lossing's Field Book of the American Revolution.*)

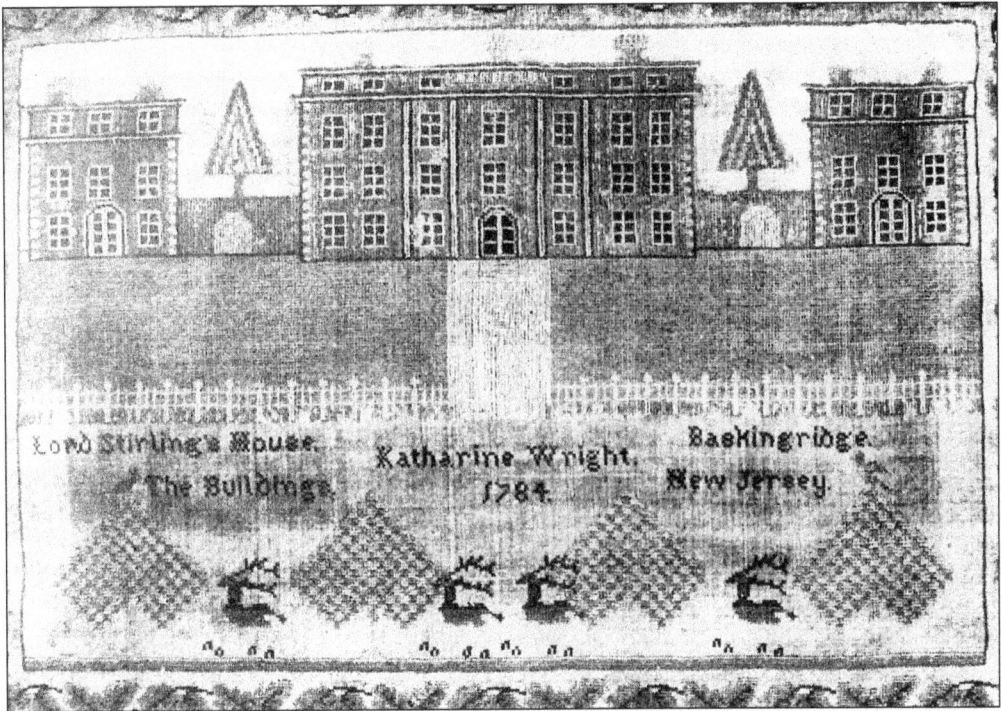

William Alexander, Lord Sterling, began construction of his mansion in 1761, but it was never completed because of the Revolutionary War and the ruinous effect it had on his finances. Nevertheless, the Basking Ridge estate was considered one of the most grandiose in the colonies. Sterling entertained General Washington, General Greene, and Governor Livingston here, among many others. It eventually fell into disrepair and was destroyed. (From a sampler by Katherine Wright, completed in 1784.)

The original part of the Lord Stirling School is reputed to have been built in the mid-1700s on the Stirling estate as a guesthouse. During those times, when the British occupied Elizabethtown and New Brunswick, there were many refugees living in safe areas of northern and western Somerset County. (Lord Stirling School.)

General Dickinson, commander of the New Jersey Militia, was stationed in the vicinity of Millstone during the spring of 1777. On January 20, 1777, a British foraging party from New Brunswick sought to obtain flour from the mills on the Millstone River. Four hundred New Jersey militiamen and fifty Pennsylvania riflemen completely routed the enemy. (Old Barracks Museum.)

This is a later mill built at Weston near the site of the Van Nest mill, where the skirmish occurred on January 20, 1777. The Weston bridge was guarded by three British cannons. The militia waded the river in January to flank the British. The mill was down a lane hedged in by osage orange trees, and a long line of fully laden British supply wagons were headed down the lane when the militia shot the lead horses, trapping the entire train. (Rutgers Library Special New Jersey Collection.)

40

General Dickinson wrote this letter to Colonel John Nielson, giving an account of the engagement at the Weston mill. He states that the skirmish lasted 20 minutes, and the militia captured 107 horses, 49 wagons, 115 cattle, 70 sheep, 106 bags of flour, and 49 prisoners. Five Americans and 30 British and Hessians were killed. As a result of this, Dickinson was promoted to major general. (Harry Kels Swan Collection.)

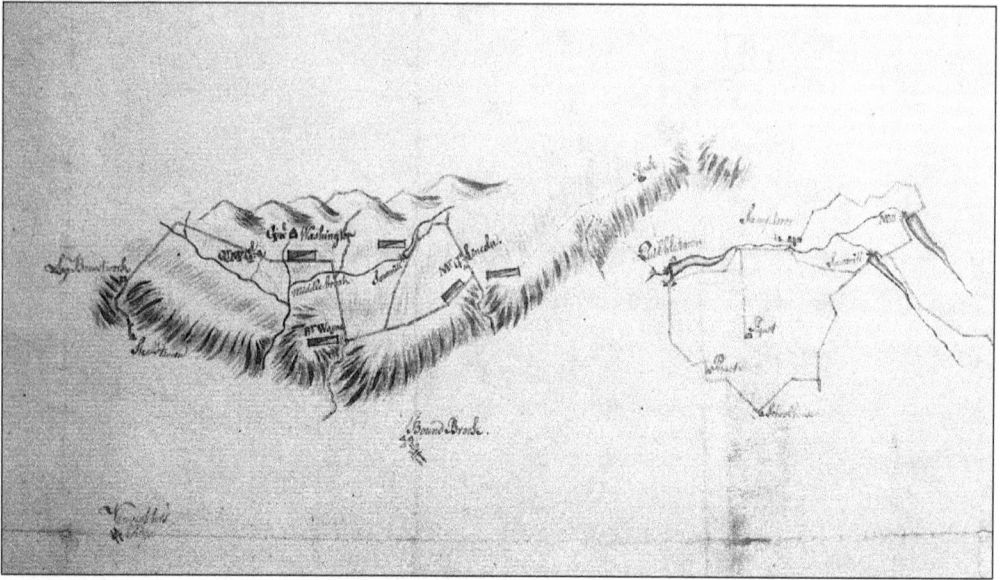

Robert Erskine, surveyor general for General Washington, drew this map of the first Middlebrook encampment for Lighthorse Harry Lee in 1777. General Washington's marquee (tent) may be seen in the Washington Valley, and the positions of Anthony Wayne and Benjamin Lincoln's troops are shown. (Harry Kels Swan Collection.)

The old Chimney Rock Tavern is reported to have hosted General Anthony Wayne and his officers during the first Middlebrook encampment. When this photo was taken by Fred N. Voorhees in 1900, the tavern had already fallen into a state of disrepair. It no longer exists. (Somerset County Historical Society.)

42

Major General Israel Putnam (left), commander of the Connecticut Line, was camped near Princeton during the first Middlebrook encampment. Major Aaron Burr (right) was one of his aids, having graduated from Princeton in 1772 at the age of 16. Burr could be seen regularly galloping up the roads of Somerset County. Mellick wrote that "the dangerously handsome Major Aaron Burr set many a Somerset maiden's heart a-fluttering, hoping for a passing smile." (David Memorial Library.)

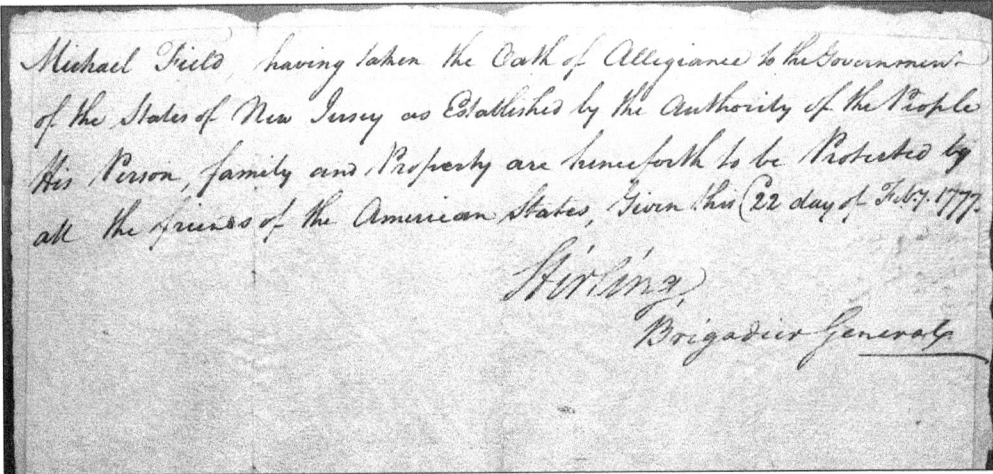

This pass certifies that Michael Field, a miller from Bound Brook, had taken the oath of allegiance to the state of New Jersey. It is signed by Brigadier General William Alexander, Lord Stirling, on February 22, 1777, while he was quartered at the Philip Van Horn House in Bridgewater. (Swan Historical Foundation.)

In 1754, the following advertisement was featured in the *New York Gazette*: "A Compleat [sic] Mill, the house 60 by 40 feet with two Pairs of Stones, and with Room for a Third, or Convenience for a Fulling Mill under the same Roof, either of which will be erected at the Expense of the Owner, situate in the County of Somerset . . . near the North Branch of the Rariton River, on a large Stream . . ." (Branchburg Historical Society.)

The mill was rented, and later purchased, by Andrew Leake, who named the location Bromley. His mill supplied flour to General Washington's army, which was camped at Pluckemin after the Battle of Princeton in January 1777. Later that year, when he heard that a British foraging party was headed his way, Leake dumped all his flour and grain into the river to prevent it from being captured. In reprisal, the British burned the mills and gave the village the new name of Burnt Mills. (Branchburg Historical Society.)

This view of the Burnt Mills dam across the Lamington River was taken in 1902 by Pluckemin photographer Edythe (Lane) Van Doren. Some sections of the dam still remain. (Peapack Gladstone Cultural and Heritage Commission.)

This photograph, taken between 1903 and 1909, shows the mill after it was rebuilt following the Civil War. A sideshot mill, it stood on the south side of the Lamington River, just west of its junction with the North Branch. The old road passed in front of the mill, but the new road and the existing bridge would have passed just to the left of this photograph. The mill was demolished in 1928. (Clarence Dillon Memorial Library.)

This is the 18th-century miller's house at Burnt Mills. During the second Middlebrook encampment, it was used as the headquarters of Clothier General James Mease. Mease was a Philadelphia merchant whose commission it was to provide clothing for Washington's army. (Branchburg Historic Preservation Commission.)

This house was once the grain barn for the mill at Burnt Mills. It was located directly across the street from the mill. Remains of the mill race may still be seen. (Branchburg Historical Society.)

Extract of a Letter from Col Matt.w Irwin D Commissary
General to John Chaloner Commissary to Gen.l Warners
Brigade Dated . Morristown . March 3.d 1777

I have acquainted his Excellency with the
purport of your letter relative to Fields Mill he desires
she may be immediately set agoing, but care must be take.n
that much flour may not be there at any time
True Copy John Chaloner Commiss.y

It is the orders of the Honble . Major General Lincoln
that Mr Fields Mills be immediately set agoing and
that no person whatever prevent or obstruct him in
bringing the Stones and materials to said Mill
by desire of Major Gen.l Lincoln
J Chaloner Commiss.y

Middlebrook march 5 1777

As a result of the depredations of the British foraging parties, General Washington ordered that the mills be cleaned out to prevent flour and grain from falling into enemy hands. This order to "set a going" Field's mill in Bound Brook originated with "his Excellency" (George Washington) and was implemented by order of Major General Benjamin Lincoln, as signed by one of his aides. (Harry Kels Swan Collection.)

Bound brook Apr. 6.th 1777

D.r General

I here with send Joseph arrow. Smith — supposed to be the Smith accused by Molesworth of being concerned with him in the Plot against the State of Pennsylvania the light horse men are to escort him to Philadelphia they will want your honours order for a guard this night

I am dear Sir your most Hum Servant —
B Lincoln

This letter from General Benjamin Lincoln at Bound Brook to General Israel Putnam near Princeton was written just a week before the Battle of Bound Brook. Lincoln requests that Putnam post a guard on Joseph Arrowsmith, a spy that had been captured and was being sent to Philadelphia. (Swan Historical Foundation.)

Shown here are Major General Benjamin Lincoln (left) and Anthony Wayne (right), who was promoted to brigadier general by Congress on February 19, 1777, while he was at Middlebrook. Around Somerset County, he was known as "Dandy Wayne" because of his good looks and fancy uniforms. (Lincoln portrait by Charles Wilson Peale, Independence National Historic Park; Wayne Portrait from *Scribner's History of the United States*, 1879.)

General Lincoln made his headquarters in the Philip Van Horne House in Bridgewater. At times, General Wayne was also quartered here. Van Horne, a judge of the Court of Common Pleas who had been a colonel during the French and Indian Wars, played both sides of the street. Horne had five beautiful daughters who were courted by officers from both armies. From January through June 1777, they accepted the protection of the British in New Brunswick, leaving their vacant house to be used by the American army. The small wing on the left was the Revolutionary War-era home. (Somerset County Historical Society.)

The Peter Williams House may have been the most pretentious one in Bound Brook at the time of the Revolution. It became known as the "Battery House" because adjacent to it was constructed the Half Moon Battery, a crescent-shaped earthworks that guarded the bridges over the Raritan River and Bound Brook. American officers were quartered in the house, which was destroyed in the early part of this century. (Somerset County Historical Society.)

This stone bridge was built to cross the bound brook in 1731. The Half Moon Battery was intended to protect Bound Brook from assault across this bridge or the Queen's Bridge over the Raritan. Hessian Captain von Ewald stormed the bridge and battery at the beginning of the Battle of Bound Brook on April 12, 1777, under "murderous fire." Of his advanced guard of 30 Jagers, only he and 10 men managed to get across this bridge; they would have had to retreat if not for Colonel von Donop's arrival at Queen's Bridge with a much larger force. When the railroad was built, Bound Brook was diverted so it would no longer pass under this bridge. The bridge still exists, but is mostly buried in the ground between the tracks. (Somerset County Historical Society.)

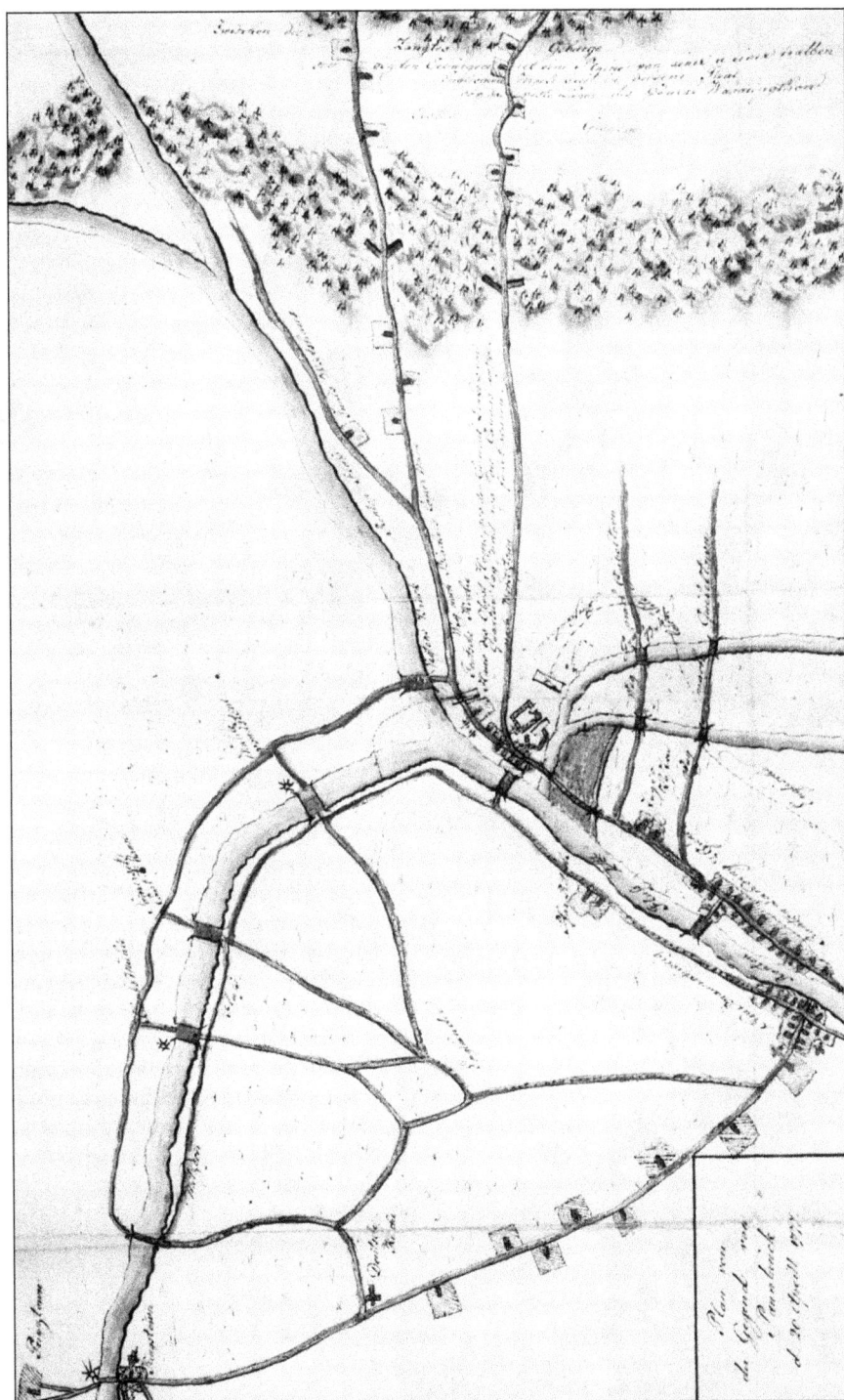

This map, drawn by Hessian Captain von Ewald, shows the area of Bound Brook at the time of the battle. In the center, by the two bridges, is the Half Moon Battery; just above that is the Van Horn House (Haus des Oberst Horns), which was identified as General Lincoln's quarters. (Johann von Ewald's Diary.)

This portrait on the upper left, showing Colonel Carl Emil Ulrich von Donop in his hunting attire, was painted just before he left for America. Von Donop was in the Trenton area at the time of the American victory, but he managed to escape. He was stationed in New Brunswick during the spring of 1777. Later that year, his regiment was badly mauled, and he was killed in the Battle of Redbank. Colonel Wilhelm von Lossberg (upper right) was a Hessian regimental commander in New Brunswick in the spring of 1777. In 1782, he became commander-in-chief of all Hessian forces in America. Hessian Captain Johann von Ewald (bottom) kept a diary of his experiences in the American Revolution, from which we have learned details we might not otherwise know. This picture was made 30 years after the war, when he had become a lieutenant general in service of Denmark. (Somerset County Library.)

Ma belle Amie.

Avant que je quitte votre Voisinage, Ma chère; je me recommande a votre bien-
veillance, et peut-être est cette Occasion qui se trouve par hasard, l'unique dans une
temps prerogue pour toujours mois. Terrible Sort pour moi! de se trouver dans un état, qui
est la mienne. Il faut que je quitte Celle, que j'aime surtout de mon Sang et de ma vie,
et au comble de mon malheur cette voiage me mets dans l'état fatal de tout le monde
de n'avoir point des nouvelles d'ici une temps qui est pour moi un Riel, de mon adorable
Nany. Hélas! ma chère. Restés la mienne, Conservés pour moi votre bien Souvenir et
un Prise de celui, qui vous aimera et adorera jusqu'au tombeau. Pardonnés ma chère
que mon lettre est si courte, je suis entouré d'un dixième officier, et le bas officier,
qui vous remets cette lettre, est recommandé par le Capit: v. Wreden et le Lt: Colonelle,
et qui est pressé. Présentés mes très humble Respects à madame votre mère et à
toutes les Demoiselles vos Sœurs. Je vous baise vos belles mains cent mille fois,
et je resterai avec la veneration la plus grande et avec un attachement inviolable.

                                    Mon adorable N— —

a 9 July,
1777.

adieu! adieu! ma chère, je vous prie
a tout de ma vie, de ne pas m'oublies.
Adieu. Hélas adieu. O! Dieu! dans
quel état je me trouve.

                         votre très humble Serviteur
                         et vrai adorateur
                         Ewald

Hessian Captain Johann von Ewald fell in love with Jeanette Van Horne, the daughter of Philip Van Horne, who, during the spring of 1777, was living in New Brunswick, under the protection of the British. This is one of a number of love letters from von Ewald to Jeanette Van Horne written during that period. They were written in French, the language commonly used between the British and Hessians. (Library of Congress, Manuscript Division.)

On Palm Sunday, April 13, 1777, Lord Cornwallis launched a four-pronged attack on the village of Bound Brook in an attempt to capture Major General Benjamin Lincoln and Brigadier General Anthony Wayne, who made their headquarters in this house (the home of Philip Van Horne), just west of town. On that date, General Lincoln was quartered there, but General Wayne was not. The Van Hornes, who had loyalist leanings, were enjoying the protection of the British in New Brunswick. (Somerset County Historical Society.)

British and Hessian troops began to leave New Brunswick in the middle of the night. Fifty horse and three battalions moved through Hillsborough to cross the Raritan River at Finderne and approached the house from the west. Colonel von Donop led 50 dragoons, 400 Hessian grenadiers, and 4 field pieces up Easton Avenue to the Queen's Bridge. General Grant marched the Jagers, the Guards Brigade, 4 four-pounders, and 2 amusettes up what is now Route 18 to the bridge over Bound Brook, and Major Maitland took 2 companies of light infantry through Quibbletown and Greenbrook to cut off the possibility of retreat. (Brigade of the American Revolution.)

54

The Van Horne House was guarded by 3 four-pounders mounted on the hill, overlooking the road. The cannons were manned by continental soldiers of the Pennsylvania Line. The attack upon the Half Moon Battery by von Ewald (under Grant) and von Donop was intended to distract the main American garrison in Bound Brook, while the American generals were being captured. (Wayne Daniels Collection.)

Sentries failed to alert headquarters of the approaching British, and the enemy column was within sight of the house when the alarm was sounded. As von Ewald wrote in his diary, General Lincoln was forced to flee without his britches. Major Maitland failed to arrive in time to prevent his escape. Von Ewald wrote that "Afterwards [Bound Brook] was ransacked and plundered because all the inhabitants were rebellious-minded." (Author's Collection.)

British and Hessian troops were harassed by American fire as they marched back to New Brunswick after the Battle of Bound Brook. A nearly spent American musket ball pierced this pewter ink pot, dated 1769 and signed "B.H." (Ben Hull) that sat on a table in a home on River Road, near Raritan Landing. (Swan Historical Foundation.)

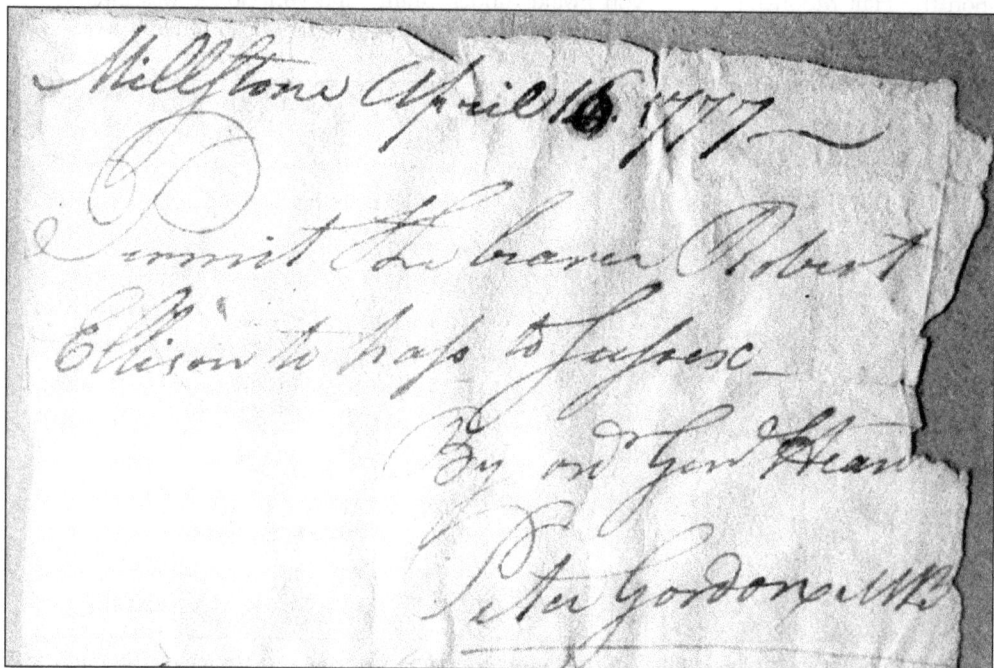

The day after the Battle of Bound Brook, Pennsylvania teamster Robert Ellison was given this pass and sent to Sussex to pick up provisions for the garrison at Bound Brook, to replace those that were captured by the British. When he returned two days later, the same pass was used with the "4" in the date changed to a "6." (Harry Kels Swan Collection.)

56

Aaron Lane was a colonial clockmaker, silversmith, and engraver in Elizabeth, NJ. When forays out of Staten Island by Hessian General von Knyphausen in 1777 made life there too dangerous, Lane sought refuge with a relative in Bound Brook. Lane is known to have made three fine, tall-case grandfather clocks in Bound Brook during the war; each one took about eight months to build. This one, made for Michael Field, commemorates the Battle of Bound Brook. Flames are engraved on each side of the maker's name, and seen near the numbers 10 and 50 are drops of blood and tears. (Harry Kels Swan Collection.)

The Middlebrook Hotel, shown here, was the first hotel in Bound Brook. Various officers were quartered here during the two Middlebrook encampments. The first Masonic Lodge in Somerset County was organized here during the Revolution by Dr. William McKissack. General Washington attended its meetings. The building has since been destroyed. (Somerset County Historical Society.)

This home, known as the Merlette House, is said to have been erected in 1700, making it one of the first houses in Bound Brook. It was once owned by Israel Harris, sheriff of Somerset County. The home was demolished in the late 1960s. (Somerset County Historical Society.)

The Van Court House was built in 1720 by Daniel Van Court. It was located on Main Street in Bound Brook, near the corner of Church Street. (Somerset County Historical Society.)

Built by Hendrick Harpending in 1720, the Frelinghuysen Tavern was where Hendrick Fisher, president of the Provincial Congress of New Jersey, read the Declaration of Independence soon after July 4, 1776. The crowd listening went wild with joy, carrying Fisher around on their backs. Cannons were fired, and the Presbyterian church bells tolled. "Rousing toasts were drunk by the lusty patrons gathered" at the tavern. (Somerset County Historical Society.)

This house was built prior to 1735. It stood on the south side of Main Street, opposite Lamont Avenue in Bound Brook. During the Revolution, it was the Samuel Swan House. Later it was purchased by Dr. William McKissack, who founded the first Masonic Lodge in Somerset County (see p. 58). The house was still standing in 1893, but has subsequently been destroyed. (Somerset County Historical Society.)

This photograph, taken c. 1900, shows all that was left of the house built by Ebenezer Trembly in 1720 at the corner of High and East Streets in Bound Brook. At the time of his death, it was owned by his son Peter. (Somerset County Historical Society.)

The Washington Camp Ground Association maintains a park on Hillcrest Road in Bridgewater on the site of one of the campgrounds associated with the Middlebrook encampment. Each Fourth of July, the Declaration of Independence is read aloud here to commemorate its first reading by Hendrick Fisher in front of the Harpending House Hotel on Main Street in Bound Brook. Fisher was then the president of the Provincial Congress of New Jersey. (Author's Collection.)

On June 14, 1777, Congress adopted the 13-star flag. It first flew over American troops here at Middlebrook. This Revolutionary-era flag is believed to display the correct alignment of stars as actually designed by Betsy Ross, rather than the circle pattern, as seen in the photograph at the top of the page. It may be seen at Patullo's Tavern in Bound Brook. (Herbert Patullo Collection.)

General Howe's Forces in New Brunswick During the Spring of 1777

16th Mounted Regiment of Light Dragoons	300
1st Battalion of Foot Guards	
2nd Battalion Coldstream Guards	945
3rd Battalion of Foot Guards	
1st, 2nd, and 3rd Battalions of Light Infantry	1424
1st and 2nd Battalions of Grenadiers	1271
The 1st Brigade of Foot, consisting of:	
4th Regiment of Foot (The King's Own)	352
23rd Regiment of Foot (The Royal Welsh Fusiliers)	416
28th Regiment of Foot	379
49th Regiment of Foot	400
The 2nd Brigade of Foot, consisting of:	
5th Regiment of Foot	400
10th Regiment of Foot	300
27th Regiment of Foot (Enniskillens)	333
40th Regiment of Foot	320
55th Regiment of Foot	274
The 3rd Brigade of Foot, consisting of:	
15th Regiment of Foot	378
17th Regiment of Foot	233
42nd Regiment of Foot (The Black Watch)	624
44th Regiment of Foot	366
The 4th Brigade of Foot, consisting of:	
33rd Regiment of Foot	363
37th Regiment of Foot	362
46th Regiment of Foot	335
64th Regiment of Foot	446
The 5th Brigade, consisting of:	
71st Regiment Scots (Highland Brigade)	1218
Chasseurs (Ferguson's Rifles) (Loyalists)	130
Queen's Rangers (Loyalists)	278
Sappers	210
von Donop's Brigade (Hessian), consisting of:	
Grenadier Battalion von Linsing	425
Grenadier Battalion von Minnigerode	446
Grenadier Battalion von Lengerke	420
Stirn's Brigade (Hessian), consisting of:	
Regiment von Lieb	710
Musketeer Regiment von Donop	624
Musketeer Regiment von Mirbach	705
von Loos' Brigade (Hessian), consisting of:	
1st Company of Hesse-Cassel Jagers	
2nd Company of Hesse-Cassel Jagers	594
Company of Anspach Jagers	
The pitiful remains of the Fusilier Regiments von Lossberg and von Knyphausen, and Grenadier Regiment von Rall, defeated at Trenton	517
Total Strength (not including artillery)	**16,498**

This is a section of the Old York Road. The alignment of the road was changed during the 1800s, leaving this section looking like all the roads in Somerset County during the American Revolution. British General Howe had 16,000 soldiers in New Brunswick during the spring of 1777. He wanted to capture our capital of Philadelphia, as he believed that doing so would end the war. His problem was that, over roads like this, a column of 16,000 men would extend over 12 miles, making them very vulnerable to sniper fire. (Author's Collection.)

This colonial-era bridge still stands where the altered course of the road no longer passes over it. General Howe knew that he would take heavy losses if he tried to march his army to Philadelphia over roads and bridges such as these, so he conceived a plan. If Washington could be lured out of his secure position in the Watchung Mountains to fight on the level fields of Franklin Township, he could be defeated, leaving the path to Philadelphia open. (Author's Collection.)

63

On June 13, 1777, General Sir William Howe (above), the commander-in-chief of all British forces in North America, and his subordinate, Lieutenant General Charles (right), Lord (Earl) Cornwallis, moved two-thirds of their army (about 11,000 men) from New Brunswick to the fields of Franklin and Hillsborough Townships. (Howe portrait from *Scribner's History of the United States*, 1897; Cornwallis portrait, Harry Kels Swan Collection.)

The Annie Van Liew House (presently the Franklin Inn) in East Millstone became the quarters for various British officers, including Howe and Cornwallis. Today, the structure houses a used book store and is open to the public. (Somerset County Historical Society.)

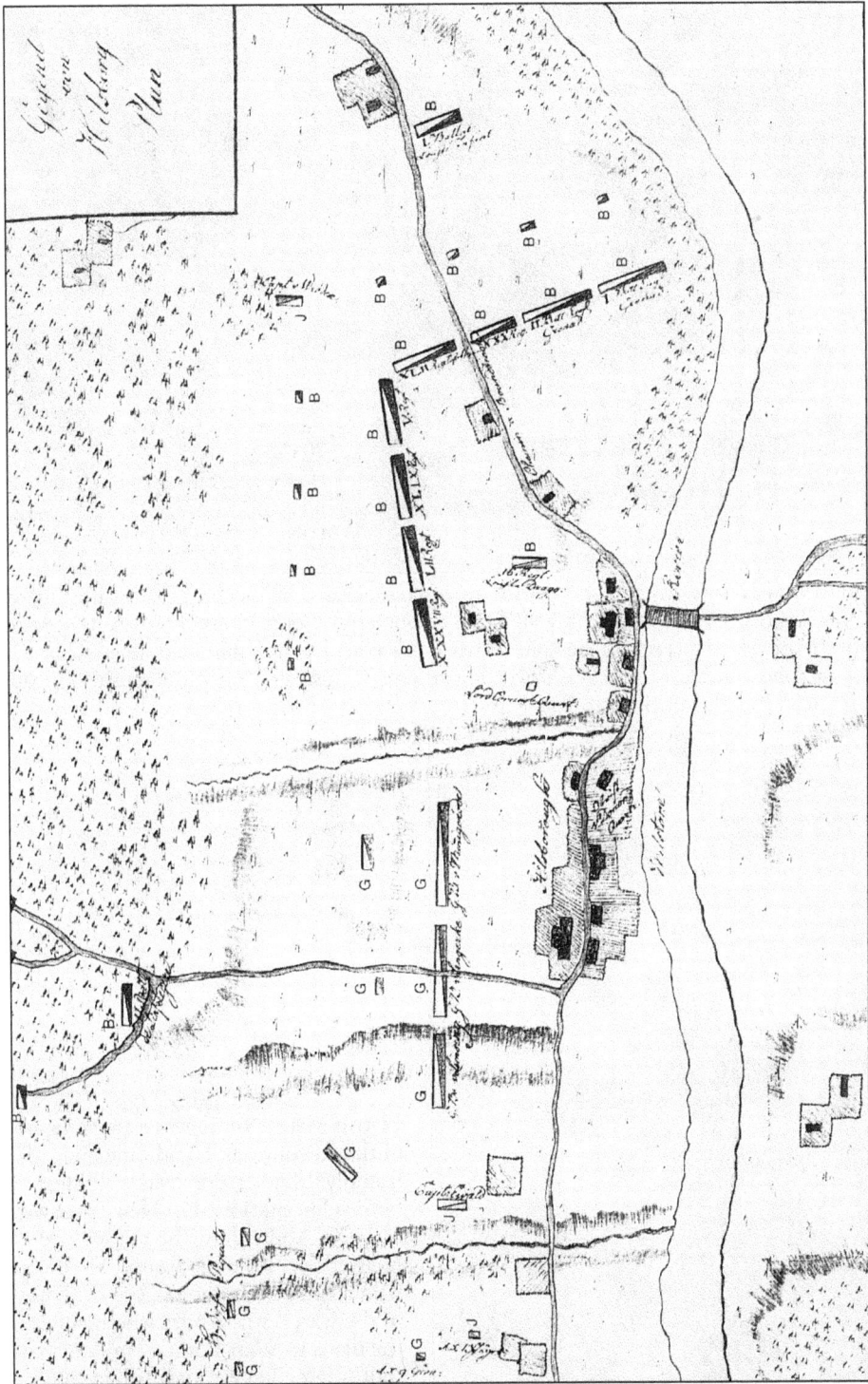

This plan of "Hilsborg" (Hillsborough), drawn by Hessian Captain Johann von Ewald. shows the 1st Division under Lord Cornwallis deployed around the village of Somerset Court House (Millstone) on June 13, 1777. (Johann Ewald's Diary.)

On June 13, 1777, one-third of the British army, commanded by General Cornwallis, marched from New Brunswick down the Amwell Road to Somerset Court House (Millstone). Another third of the British army, under Hessian General de (von) Heister, marched down what is now Easton Avenue and De Mott Lane to his encampment, just west of Middlebush. (Brigade of the American Revolution.)

British Major Andre was a tragic figure of the Revolution. Handsome and friendly, Major Andre was well liked by both sides. Stationed in New Brunswick in 1777, Andre drew the maps of De Heister's deployment around Middlebush, which can be seen on pp. 68–69. Later in the war, it was Andre who received the plans to West Point from American traitor Benedict Arnold. When Major Andre was caught in civilian clothes and hung as a spy, even Washington grieved. (Swan Historical Foundation.)

Hessian grenadiers wore long-skirted, blue coats with a yellow waistcoat extending below the hips, and yellow breeches gathered at the knee by black gaiters. Their hair was drawn back into a tail that hung nearly to their waist and was covered by a thick paste of tallow and flour. Their mustaches would have been stiffened with a black paste. An English officer wrote that the brass hats and swords of the Brunswick Dragoons were as heavy as the whole equipment of a British soldier. (Wayne Daniels Collection.)

This drawing of Hessian Jagers was made during the Revolution. Jager, meaning "hunter," was the German name for a light infantry soldier. When it became apparent that Washington (with half as many men) would not be goaded into a fight, the British army returned to New Brunswick on June 19, 1777. Von Ewald wrote the following in his diary: "On this march all the plantations of the disloyal inhabitants, numbering perhaps some fifty persons, were sacrificed to fire and devastation." (David Memorial Library.)

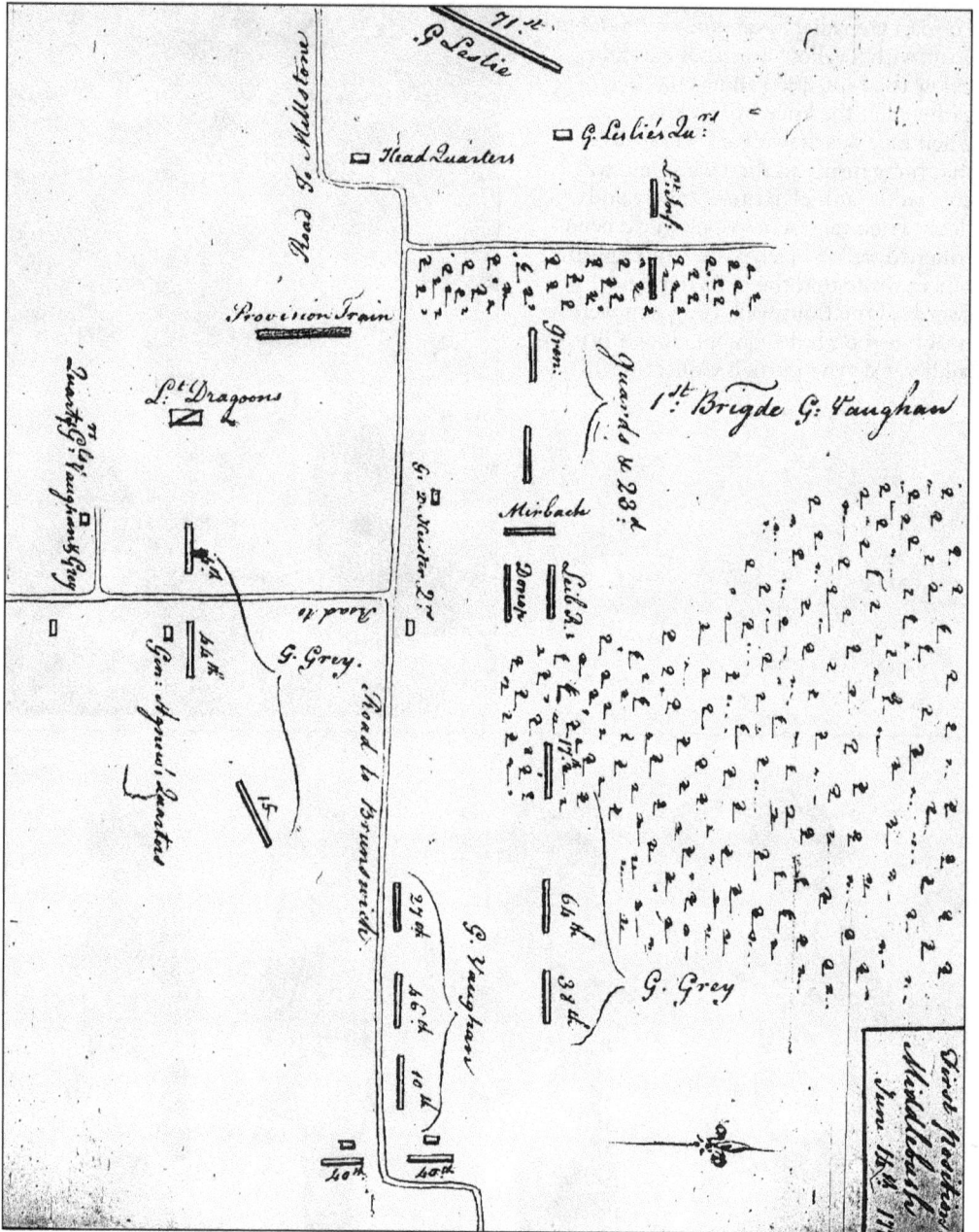

This is Major Andre's map of the first deployment of British and Hessian troops under de Heister at Middlebush on June 14, 1777. (Major Andre's Diary.)

This is Major Andre's map of the second deployment of British and Hessian troops under de Heister at Middlebush on June 15, 1777. (Major Andre's Diary.)

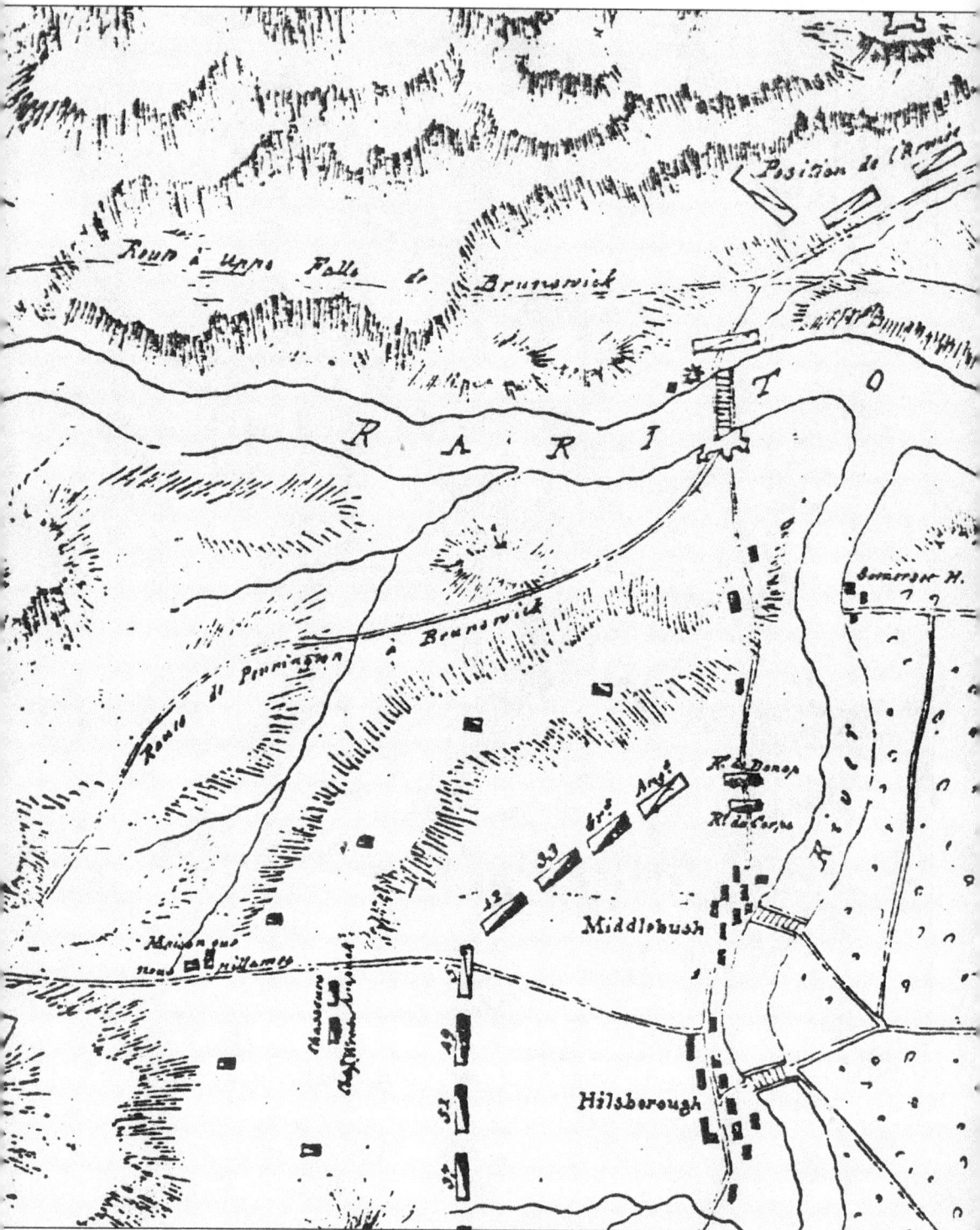

This map by Hessian Jager Lieutenant V. Wangenheim purports to show the positions of the British and American armies on June 15, 1777. Note that Hillsborough and Middlebush are shown as towns on the Hillsborough side of the Millstone River, and Somerset Court House

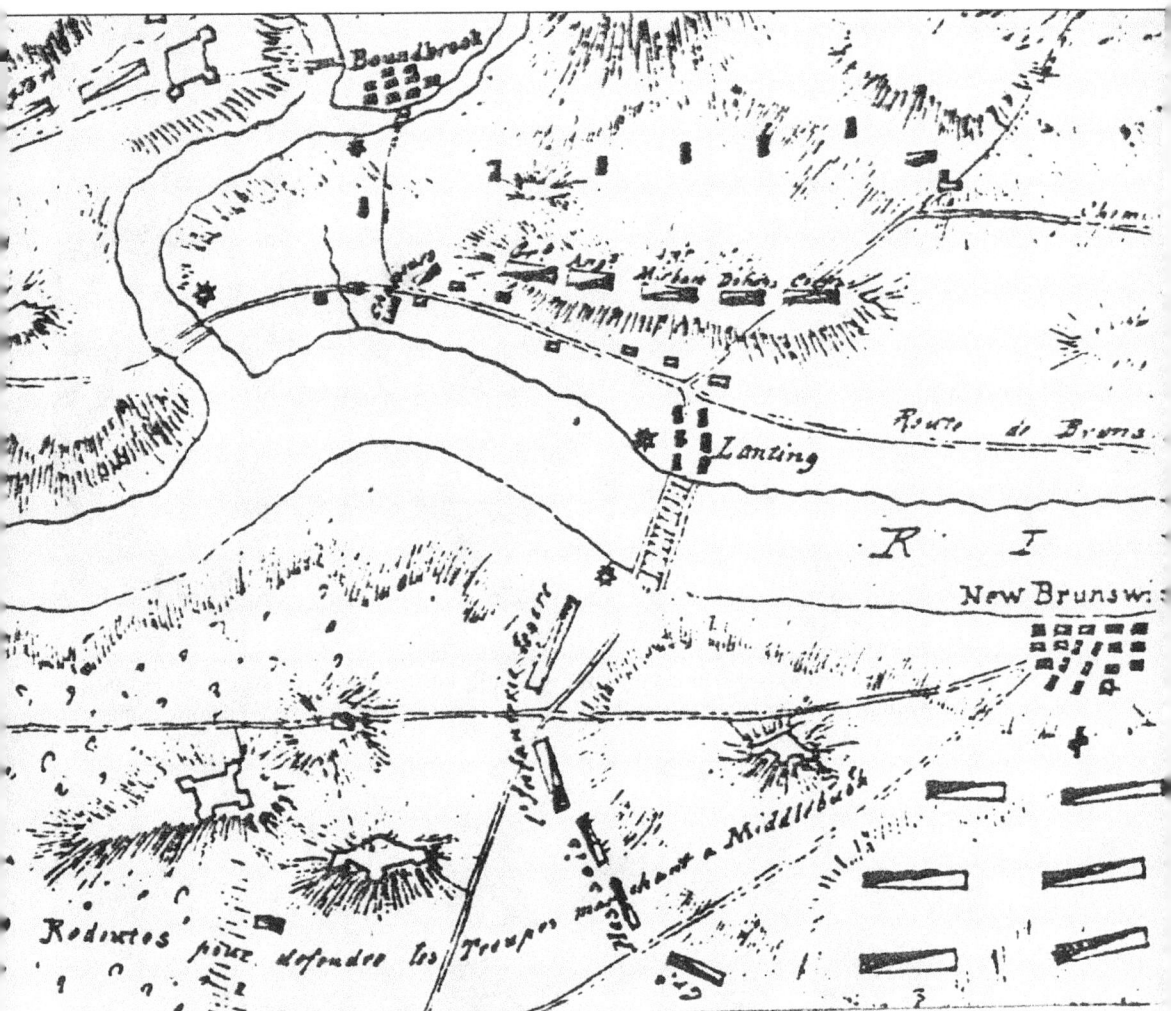

is shown on the Franklin side of the river. These are the kinds of maps commanders were sometimes forced to work with. (Morristown National Historic Park.)

The Jacobus Wyckoff House in Franklin Park was built between 1745 and 1766. The house is shown on the map made by Washington's surveyor general, Robert Erskine. (Historic American Buildings Survey 447, 1937.)

The Cornelius Stoothoof House, built in the mid-1700s on South Middlebush Road, was just far enough outside Middlebush to avoid burning by the British and Hessians as they returned to New Brunswick on June 19, 1777. Cornelius Stoothoof was a private in the Somerset County Militia, where he served as an express rider. (Historic American Buildings Survey 674, 1941.)

The old Veghte homestead was located between Middlebush and Griggstown. It is typical of the homes erected by the Dutch during the colonial period. Henry Veghte served as a private in the Somerset County Militia. (Rutgers Special New Jersey Collection.)

This is one of Franklin Township's beautiful, old Dutch barns. Von Ewald wrote in his diary that "the enemy had also hidden several times in the barn of the preacher (Rev. Abraham Beach, Rector of Christ Church in New Brunswick) across the river (in Franklin) and fired on my quarters (in Piscataway) through holes cut in the barn walls." (Rutgers Special New Jersey Collection.)

This house was built by Symen Van Wickle in 1722, on land in Franklin Township that he inherited from his father, Evert Van Wickelen. Symen's son Nicholas most likely owned it at the time of the Revolution. Today, it belongs to the Meadows Foundation and is open to the public. (Historic American Buildings Survey 479, 1938.)

The Aaron Hageman House in Franklin was built in the 1770s. Aaron enlisted as a private in the Somerset County Militia and rose to the rank of sergeant. (Historic American Buildings Survey 620, 1939.)

This is the home of John Honeyman in Griggstown, Franklin Township. A former British army officer, Honeyman played the part of a Tory in order to spy for Washington. His information helped Washington plan the Battle of Trenton. Once, while he was away from home, a mob threatened to burn his house down. His wife produced a letter of protection signed by George Washington and the crowd dispersed. (Rutgers Special New Jersey Collection.)

After the war, Washington's spy, John Honeyman, moved to Lamington in Bedminster Township, where his grave may be seen in the Presbyterian church cemetery. (Rutgers Special New Jersey Collection.)

Jane McCrea, daughter of Reverend James McCrea of Bedminster, was engaged to marry an officer serving with British General Burgoyne in upstate New York. Miss McCrea was murdered and scalped by Iroquois Scouts employed by the British, who were supposed to be escorting her to meet her betrothed. The incident infuriated settlers in that area and contributed to the defeat of General Burgoyne. Until the end of the 19th century, this incident was considered so important as to require inclusion in any history of the Revolution. This lithograph was made by Nathaniel Currier in 1846. (New York Historical Society.)

Three

FROM 1778 TO 1779

The American army dogs the British march from Philadelphia to New York, forcing a show-down at Monmouth. Washington spends the winter at the Wallace House during the second Middlebrook encampment. British Lieutenant Colonel John Simcoe leads the Queen's Rangers on a raid into Somerset County.

BANNER OF WASHINGTON'S LIFE GUARD.

The commander-in-chief's guard, commonly called "the Life Guard," was an elite corps assigned to protect General Washington; it also fought in battle. Members were selected based on superior physical, moral, and intellectual character. At the time of the second Middlebrook encampment, the guard (consisting of 180 men) camped at the Wallace House. This is a representation of their banner. (*Lossing's Field Book of the American Revolution*, 1859.)

In 1778, General Howe was recalled to England to explain his lack of success. General Sir Henry Clinton (shown here) took command of all British forces. Clinton wanted to move his army from Philadelphia to New York. Ignoring General Howe's warnings, Clinton decided to move his troops by land across New Jersey. His column stretched out for over 12 miles and moved very slowly. The British and Hessian soldiers were carrying heavy loads. Temperatures reached 92 degrees in the shade. Americans stopped up all the wells in the path of the British army. (New York Historical Society.)

General Washington and his army crossed the Delaware at Coryell's Ferry (Lambertville) and followed to the north of the British army, passing through Somerset County along what is now Route 518 in Montgomery Township. This well, known as "Washington's well," alongside Route 518, was drunk dry by the men and horses of Washington's army during that march. (Rutgers Special New Jersey Collection.)

Daniel Morgan was born in Hunterdon County, NJ, in 1736. After a quarrel with his father, he left home to seek his fortune on the Virginia frontier. He became a skilled "Indian fighter" during the French and Indian War. In 1778, he was a captain in the Continental army, commanding a special light infantry corps of 500 hand-picked frontiersmen known as Morgan's Riflemen. For special psychological effect, Morgan's men sometimes dressed as Indians and covered their faces with war paint, shouting war whoops as they attacked the British. Morgan became a brigadier general in 1780. (*Scribner's History of the United States*, 1879.)

This re-enactor is dressed in the garb of Morgan's Riflemen. As British General Clinton's army made its way across New Jersey, Morgan's Riflemen dogged them on the right, and New Jersey and Pennsylvania troops harassed them on the left. Finally, they were forced to stop and fight. The Battle of Monmouth on June 28, 1778, was the biggest battle of the American Revolution and an American victory. Terrible heat took its toll on both sides, and the British were permitted to withdraw to Staten Island. (Wayne Daniels Collection.)

As Washington's army traveled down what is now Route 518 in Montgomery Township on the way to the Battle of Monmouth, the soldiers passed this house. Washington spent a night here, in the home of John Price Hunt. (Author's Collection.)

Nearby, in Montgomery Township, is the 1752 Dirck Gulick House, which belongs to the Van Harlingen Historical Society and is open to the public. Abram, John, and Joakim Gulick served in the Somerset County Militia. (Author's Collection.)

Across the street from the Gulick House is the 1750 home of Peter Ditmars. Ditmars was a private in Captain Vroom's company of Somerset County Militia. (Author's Collection.)

"Honest John Hart" was a signer of the Declaration of Independence. As a result, the British put a price on his head. Hart lived in Hopewell and owned this mill in Rocky Hill. In 1779, he died of exposure while hiding out in the Sourland Mountains to elude British search parties. (Somerset County Library.)

In the mid-1770s, John and Mary (Maddox) Wallace built their retirement home in what is now Somerville. Mr. Wallace had been in the textile trade in Philadelphia and was a member of the city council there. The Wallaces were believed to have had loyalist leanings. Mr. Wallace negotiated a fee for the use of his house by General and Mrs. Washington during the second Middlebrook encampment from December 1778 through June 1779. (James Kurzenberger, State Park Service.)

The front view of the Wallace House is the side facing away from the road. The Wallaces shared the house while the Washingtons were in residence. Washington may have stayed in this home longer than anywhere else during the Revolution. His Life Guard camped on the grounds. The house has been preserved and is presently a state park that is open to the public. (Author's Collection.)

These images of George and Martha Washington give a good impression of their appearance at the time of their residence in the Wallace House. The Washingtons entertained lavishly, dining nightly with up to 30 officers or visiting dignitaries. It was here that Washington planned the Six Nations Iroquois campaign in response to massacres by the Iroquois in the Cherry Valley of New York and the Wyoming Valley of Pennsylvania. (James Kurzenberger, State Park Service.)

It was not a particularly cold winter, but years later, all Martha Washington could remember of her stay at the Wallace House was shivering under many quilts and having members of the Life Guard rush into the bedroom in the middle of the night, throw open the windows, and point their muskets into the darkness in response to a real or imagined alarm. (Author's Collection.)

Major General Benedict Arnold was among the many guests of the Washingtons at the Wallace House. Up to that point, Arnold had had a sometimes heroic and sometimes insubordinate career. About the same time, in Philadelphia, Arnold met and then married Margaret Shippen, who came from a prominent royalist family. She turned him against his country. In August 1780, Washington appointed Arnold commander of West Point. Within a month, he was caught conspiring with Major Andre to surrender the post to the British (see p. 66). (*Scribner's History of the United States*, 1879.)

This is the central hall of the Wallace House, looking toward the front door *c.* 1905. Few changes were made to the home from the time the Wallaces owned it until it was acquired by the Revolutionary Memorial Society during the 19th century. (Somerset County Historical Society.)

Alexander Hamilton distinguished himself as an artillery captain in the Battles of Long Island, White Plains, Trenton, and Princeton. General Nathaniel Greene took notice of him and introduced him to General Washington, who made Hamilton his aide-de-camp and confidential secretary in March 1777. Hamilton lived in the Wallace House with the Washingtons. (Museum of the City of New York.)

This is a view of the central hall of the Wallace House, looking toward the rear door and the stairs. The Washingtons used one room on the first floor as a parlor and one rear bedroom upstairs. Other guests included General and Mrs. Knox, General and Mrs. Greene, Baron von Steuben, Lady Stirling and her daughter Kitty, and many others. (Historic American Buildings Survey 620, 1936.)

This little wooden document box was carried by Lieutenant Colonel Dirck Middagh during the Revolutionary War. The box, covered by floral wallpaper and hinged with leather, held handmade paper, quill pens, letters and dispatches, and a small pen knife used to cut goose, swan, and crow feathers (to make writing implements). (Swan Historical Foundation.)

Dirck Middagh was a major in the 1st Battalion of the Somerset County Militia in 1776, and was promoted to lieutenant colonel in February 1777. This was his house. It is located across the street from the Wallace House, next to the Old Dutch Parsonage. It is not open to the public. (Author's Collection.)

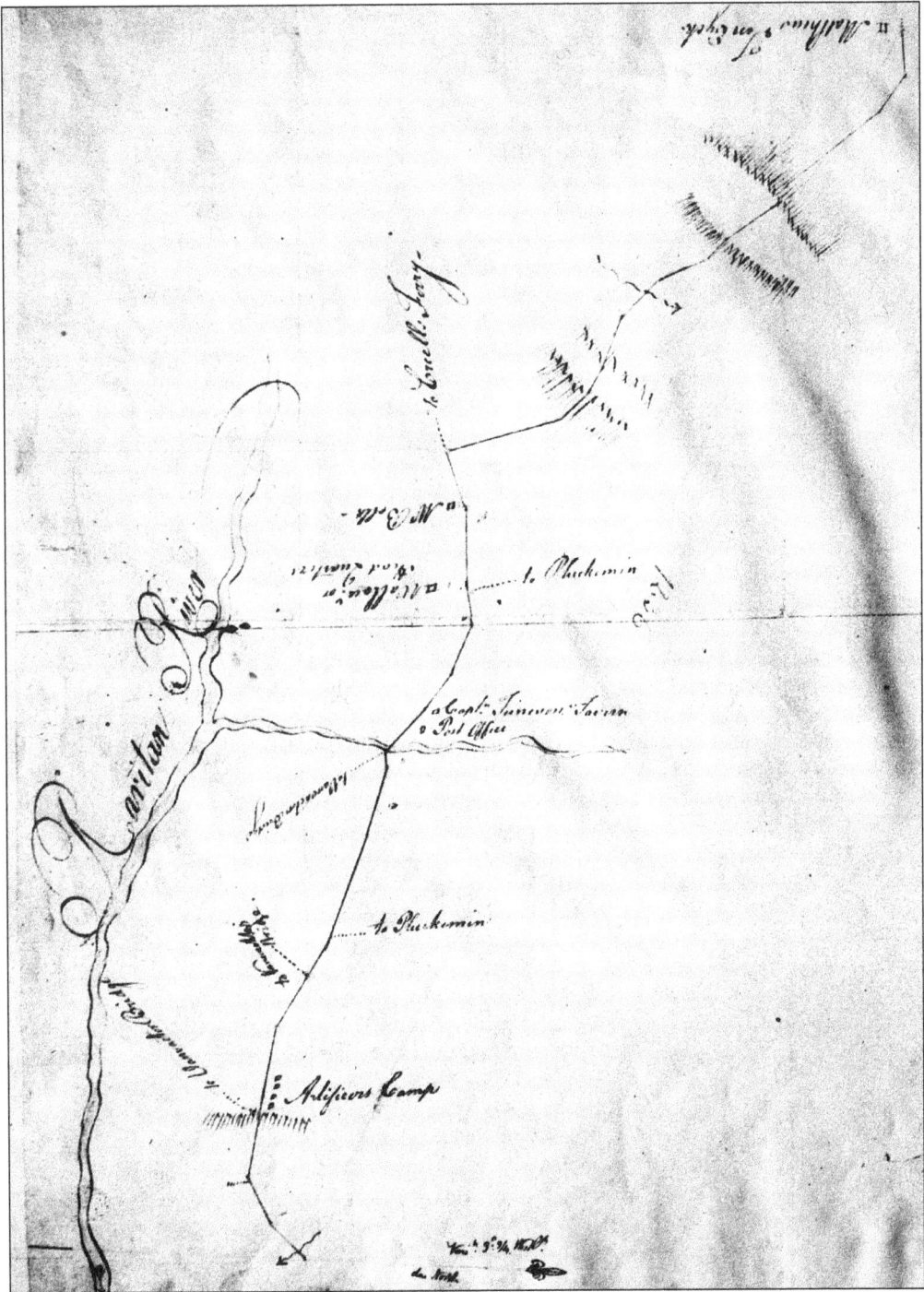

This map was drawn by Washington's map maker, Surveyor General Robert Erskine. The artificer's camp at the bottom was in Finderne. From there, the Old York Road leads past Tunison's Tavern (now Somerville) and the Wallace House, which is marked "Head Quarters." The road on the upper right is Milltown Road, which leads to Matthias Ten Eyck in North Branch. (New York Historical Society.)

Major General Nathaniel Greene and Mrs. Catharine (Littlefield) Greene became close friends of General and Mrs. Washington. Greene was made commander of the New Jersey Line following the Battle of Long Island, and was appointed quartermaster general during the second Middlebrook encampment. (General Greene photo courtesy Independence National Historic Park; Mrs. Greene photo courtesy *Century Magazine*, 1878.)

During the second Middlebrook encampment, the Greenes were quartered in the home of Dirck Van Veghten in Finderne. General Greene wrote a letter to Colonel Wadsworth about a dance he held at the house in March 1779, when General Washington "danced with Mrs. Greene for three hours without sitting down" and stated that "upon the whole, we had a pretty little frisk." (Historic American Buildings Survey 661, 1940.)

Lighthorse Harry Lee graduated from Princeton in 1774 at the age of 17. During the second Middlebrook encampment, he was in command of two troops of horse, having been promoted to major for valor in battle at the age of 22. After the war, he became governor of Virginia, a member of Congress, and the father of Robert E. Lee. (Independence National Historic Park.)

Lee was quartered at the Phillip Van Horne House, where it is said that he rode his horse in the front door and out the back. Lee developed a lifelong friendship with Mrs. Greene, and they corresponded faithfully over the years. In 1818, he died at her plantation on a sea island off the coast of Georgia, where she had died four years before. They were buried side by side in a little, stone-walled cemetery, in the midst of an olive grove surrounded by tropical flowers. His family later had him disinterred and brought back to Virginia. (Historic American Buildings Survey 523, 1938.)

Major General Baron Fredrich Wilhelm Ludolf Gerhard Augustin von Steuben had been an aide-de-camp of Frederick the Great, a high-ranking officer of the Margrave of Baden, and grand marshal of the Prince of Hohenzollern-Heckingen. He came to America to add another accomplishment to his resume but fell in love with the American cause. He later became an American citizen. (New York Historical Society.)

During the second Middlebrook encampment, Major General von Steuben was quartered in the Abraham Staats House in South Bound Brook. He had been made inspector general by George Washington at Valley Forge when he was 50 years old. (*Our Home* Magazine, 1890.)

The living room in the Abraham Staats House was used by von Steuben as his office. He wrote his *Regulations for the Infantry of the United States* here in German, and then translated it into rather poor French. A French officer named Fleury corrected it. Captain Peter DuPonceau, a 19-year-old French officer, translated it into poor English, and then American Captain Benjamin Walker corrected the English. (Rutgers Special New Jersey Collection.)

This is the kitchen in the Staats House. Washington was entertained here a number of times. On May 2, 1779, von Steuben hosted a dinner for 60 guests under a tent by the house. Guests included French Ambassador Conrad Gerard and Don Juan de Miralles, the Spanish envoy of the governor of Havana. (Rutgers Special New Jersey Collection.)

BARON VON STEUBEN REVOLUTIONARY HOME, BOUND BROOK, N. J.

Abraham Staats may have been a collector of taxes for the crown before the Revolutionary War. However, that he embraced the American cause is attested to by the fact that, when British General Howe offered amnesty to those who would swear allegiance to the crown, Staats was specifically excluded. A slave named Tory Jack, who lived in his house, pretended to have loyalist sympathies so he could go among the British soldiers and spy for the American side. (Somerset County Historical Society.)

The central part of the Staats House, described as "old" in 1738, was the only part that existed when Baron von Steuben made it his headquarters. The one-story addition on the left is a kitchen that was added in 1800, and the two-story addition on the right was erected in 1825. The house belonged to the Staats family from 1738 until 1935. This picture was taken c. 1880. (Rutgers Special New Jersey Collection.)

92

General von Steuben is credited for providing the training and discipline that turned the American troops into a cohesive fighting force. A soldier's life at camp Middlebrook was filled with drilling and inspections. On May 2, 1779, a grand parade and review of the army was held in honor of French Ambassador Conrad Gerard and visiting Spanish Envoy Don Juan de Miralles. (Brigade of the American Revolution.)

On May 14, 1779, there was a review of the army at Middlebrook by some chiefs of the Delaware Indians. General Washington rode his horse in front of the troops, who were standing at attention. Washington was followed on horseback by his slave and valet, Bill, who was said to have regarded himself as second in command. They were followed by Delaware chiefs riding bareback. (Brigade of the American Revolution.)

Henry Knox, a Boston bookseller before the war, liked to read books about artillery. During the siege of Boston in 1775, Dorchester Heights was fortified with cannons that Knox transported from Fort Ticonderoga. Washington made Knox a brigadier general in 1776 and placed him in command of the American Artillery Corps, a rank and position he held during the second Middlebrook encampment. (Independence National Historic Park.)

Brigadier General Knox and his wife, Lucy, were quartered at the Jacobus Van Der Veer House, just north of Pluckemin. In July 1779, their infant daughter Julia died. She was refused burial in the Dutch Reformed cemetery next door because the Knox family was Congregationalist. Even though he had donated the land, Jacobus Van Der Veer had also been denied burial of his daughter in the cemetery because she was insane. Van Der Veer allowed his guests to bury their daughter outside the cemetery fence, near the grave of his own daughter. (Somerset County Library.)

Much of the American artillery consisted of cannons captured at Fort Ticonderoga and in the Battle of Saratoga. Many, such as this one, were old when they were sent to the colonies during the French and Indian War. (Wayne Daniels Collection.)

Here is another of the long line of cannons drawn into Pluckemin behind teams of horses in December 1778. Today, the cannons may be seen at Fort Ticonderoga National Historic Park. (Wayne Daniels Collection.)

General Knox established the artillery school at Pluckemin. It was located in the middle of what is presently The Hills development. The building on the right, with the cupola, is the academy, which housed a single 30-by-50-foot classroom. Here, officers and men were trained in tactics, gunnery, and other military subjects. Knox had 49 companies with over 1,600 men at the artillery park. (Morristown National Historic Park.)

At the beginning of the war, artillery soldiers dressed in uniforms of the same colors as the continental line, shown above. By the time of the second Middlebrook encampment, it had been decided that the artillery would wear black coats turned up with red, white jackets and breeches, and hats trimmed with yellow. In January 1779, General Knox wrote to his brother in Boston, asking him to procure some cloth in these colors to make uniforms for himself and a staff officer. (Brigade of the American Revolution.)

King Louis XVI of France appointed Conrad Gerard, shown here, as minister plenipotentiary to the United States as the treaty of alliance was signed in the spring of 1778. In April of that year, he set sail for America in Admiral D'Estaing's flag ship, the *Languedoc*. On February 18, 1779, Ambassador Gerard was the guest of honor at a grand fete and ball hosted by General Knox and his officers to celebrate the first anniversary of the French alliance. (*Lossing's Pictorial Field Book of the Revolution.*)

The Grand Pavilion (or Palace, as General Greene called it), 100 feet long, with 13 arches supported by columns, was constructed to house the celebration. General Washington, his staff, and an escort arrived on horseback and were followed by Mrs. Washington in a coach drawn by 4 horses. There was a 13-gun salute. Seventy ladies, most of whom were from the local countryside, and over 300 gentlemen were in attendance. Grandstands were built so that local residents could view the spectacle, which included fireworks. (Private Collection.)

Major General Arthur St. Clair was a native of Edinburgh, Scotland. He had served in the British army during the French and Indian War, but chose the American side during the Revolution. He was appointed a colonel in the Continental army in January 1776, and a brigadier general in August of the same year. He was an active participant in the Battles of Trenton and Princeton, and became a major general in February 1777. (Independence National Historic Park.)

This home, located next to Sacred Heart Cemetery on Millstone River Road in Hillsborough, was built after the Revolutionary War. A wing on the back of the structure contains what remains of the house that quartered Major General Arthur St. Clair during the second Middlebrook encampment. Due to fires, all that remains of that period is the foundation, floor joists, and a beautiful cooking fireplace. (Author's Collection.)

Major General John Sullivan (left) assumed command when General Charles Lee was captured at Widow White's tavern in 1776. At Middlebrook, Sullivan was given command of the expedition against the Iroquois. The Chevalier Louis le Beque Du Portail (right) was a French engineer and officer commissioned by Congress as commandant of the corps of engineers, sappers, and miners. He brought with him experience in building bridges and fortifications. (Independence National Historic Park.)

In Bound Brook, the Fisher Hotel, also known as the Middlebrook Hotel, housed a number of officers during the second Middlebrook encampment, including Generals Sullivan and Du Portail. It was said that many bayonette marks could be seen in its low ceiling beams. The hotel has been demolished. (Somerset County Historical Society.)

At the Battle of Long Island, Colonel William Smallwood's Maryland regiment fought valiantly under Lord Stirling to cover Washington's retreat. All but 70 of Smallwood's 1,100 men were killed. At Middlebrook, Smallwood (left) was a brigadier general. He later became a major general and was elected governor of Maryland in 1785. Brigadier General Lachlan Mackintosh (right) was in command of the North Carolina troops encamped at Middlebrook. (Independence National Historic Park.)

The Middlebrook encampments included regiments from Connecticut, Delaware, Georgia, Maryland, Massachusetts, New Hampshire, New Jersey, New York, North Carolina, Pennsylvania, Rhode Island, and Virginia. (Brigade of the American Revolution.)

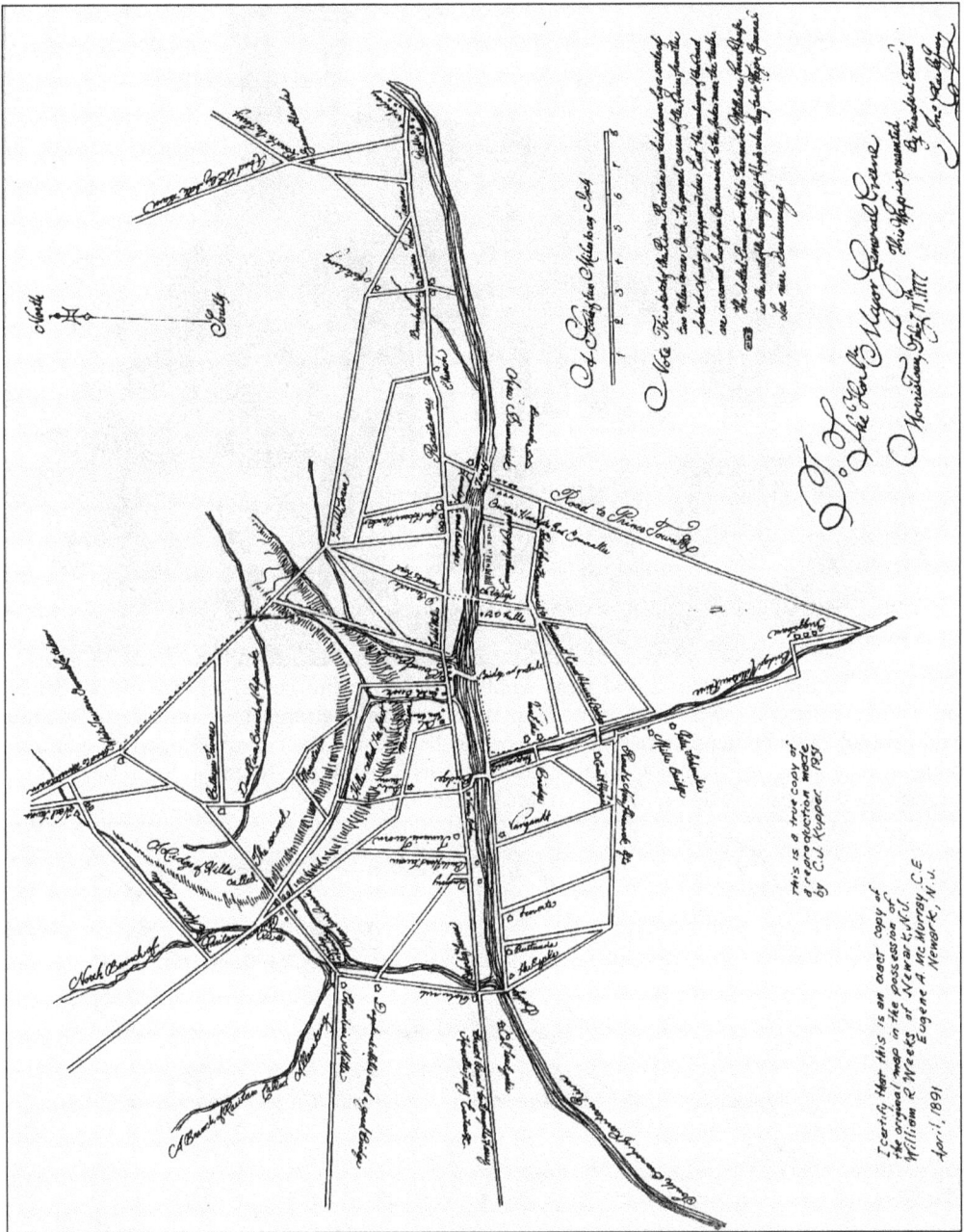

This map, made for Major General Nathaniel Greene during the first Middlebrook encampment, shows the kind of maps commanders had to work with. (Somerset County Historical Society.)

Cornelius Tunison's Tavern stood near what is presently the corner of East Main Street and Grove Street in Somerville. American officers were quartered here during the second Middlebrook encampment. After the war, Somerville became the county seat, when Tunison donated land for a courthouse and jail. Over the years, the tavern was expanded. The original structure was eventually demolished. (Private Collection.)

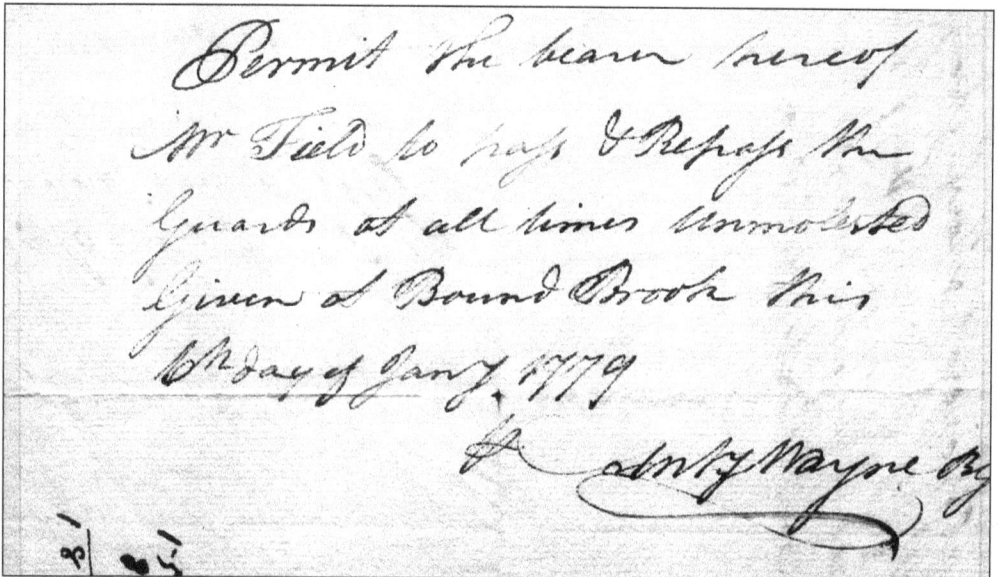

During the war, it was necessary for civilians to carry passes that permitted them to cross guard points and be identified if necessary. This pass, issued to Michael Field of Bound Brook, is signed by Brigadier General Anthony Wayne. Field, a miller, supplied flour to the Continental army. (Swan Historical Foundation.)

The earliest part of this house was built in 1763 and operated as a general store by Jacob Vosseler during the Revolution. People traveled great distances to shop here because there were so few stores. Records show that Governor Livingston bought a broom here when he was living in Basking Ridge in 1777. General and Mrs. Washington may have shopped here. Today known as the Allen Tavern, it is a private dwelling located at the intersection of Allen Road and Foothill Road in Bridgewater. (Author's Collection.)

John Brokaw was chosen to be a lieutenant in Captain Peter D. Vroom's militia company. Brokaw was killed while leading his men at the Battle of Germantown, PA. A neighbor carried him from the field and later brought his watch and sword home to his family. In the spring of 1779, George Washington rode from the Wallace House to pay his respects to the widow and express his sorrow for her bereavement. The Brokaw House still stands along the Raritan River on Milltown Road, near Route 22, in Bridgewater. (Branchburg Historical Society.)

A List of all the Persons Names who are
to bring in wheate for the Armey for the year 1779

William Lane — 40 Bushels — to be Brought to Simons mills

John Ven Nest — 6 — to be Brought to do

~~Henry D Vroom 9 to be Brought do~~

Abraham Ten Eyk — 12 — to be Brought to Bankers

Widdow Bogart — to be Brought to Simons

Peter Dumont 20 of Inden to — do

John Bogart of weat 20 & 10 of Inden to — do

~~John Ettinger 10 of wt & 25 of Inden to huff~~

Fradrick Monson — 4 of Inden to do

Joseph Stevens 8 wheat — to do

George Hall 10 of ry 10 of Inden to do

Edward Hall 50 of Corn — to huff

John Huff 5 of do — to Do

Lowrance Dumot 10 of wt & 10 of ry to do

George Hall 30 of Corn — to Simons

Wm Hall do of Corn — to do

Jacob Wickhoff 20 of Corn to do

Andris Ten Eyk 10 of wt — to Bankers

Gerrit Ferbares 60 of Inden to do

John Lane — 20 of do — to do

James D

This is a list of farmers in and around North Branch who supplied wheat and Indian corn for Washington's army in 1779, during the second Middlebrook encampment. (Rutgers Special New Jersey Collection.)

Washington's men built and lived in huts such as this during the Middlebrook encampment. Up to 12 men could live in a small cabin like this. (Wayne Daniels Collection.)

This brass cooking pot was made in Holland in the late 17th century. Passed down through the family, it was inherited by Mrs. Middagh. Her husband, Lieutenant Colonel Dirck Middagh, carried it with him during the war as his personal cooking vessel. He was commander of the 1st Battalion, Somerset County Militia, during most of the second Middlebrook encampment. This was during the time Colonel Frelinghuysen served in Congress. (Swan Historical Foundation.)

At various intervals, along the top of the Watchung Mountains, great pyramids of wood were erected as beacons. They were to be ignited as signals to indicate the approach of the British army, thus showing where the militia should assemble. This beacon fire was set during the reenactment of the Battle of Springfield. (Wayne Daniels Collection.)

Somerset County's General William Alexander, Lord (Earl) Stirling, designed the beacons. This is his drawing. They were to be 14 feet square at the bottom, stand about 20-feet high, surround a 30-foot sapling, and be filled with dried brush. During the day, to sound the alarm, signal guns were fired from the beacon posts. At Short Hills, there was an 18-pounder, affectionately known as "The Old Sow." (*Lossing's Pictorial Field-Book of the Revolution.*)

High atop the Watchung Mountains in North Plainfield and soaring almost 400 feet above the plains is Washington's Rock. Washington often came here with his telescope to reconnoiter British troop movements, or to see the British fleet in New York Harbor. It is said that he sometimes came here alone just to sit in deep thought. This was also a beacon site. This 1880 photo shows the whitewash applied every year by Civil War veteran William Pangborn. Today, the area is a state park that is open to the public. (Wesley H. Ott Collection.)

The Washington House Tavern was built in 1738 and served as a "house of entertainment" and stop along the stagecoach route from Trenton to Morristown. General Washington often stopped here for some refreshment on the way to or from nearby Washington's Rock, causing residents to dub the tavern "Washington's Headquarters." The building burned down in 1963. (Somerset County Historical Society.)

Early in the morning of October 26, 1779, British Lieutenant Colonel John Simcoe led a raid of the Queen's Rangers (American loyalist cavalry) through the Raritan Valley. His three objectives were to capture Governor Livingston, destroy a fleet of 50 large troop boats stored near Van Veghten's Bridge in Finderne, and if possible, lure the militia into an ambush. Although he attempted to impersonate Lee's Virginia Light Horse Brigade, his true identity was detected when he and his men stopped here, at the Frelinghuysen Tavern in Bound Brook. (Frederick N. Voorhees Collection.)

Simcoe expected to find Governor William Livingston quartered here, at the Phillip Van Horne House, but his information was faulty. His troops pushed on to Finderne, where they destroyed 18 boats and their traveling carriages, an ammunition wagon, some harnesses, and a quantity of forage and stores. They also burned the nearby Dutch Reformed Church. (Author's Collection.)

In 1777, Major John Graves Simcoe had been given command of the Queen's Rangers. He quickly rose to the rank of lieutenant colonel. Simcoe was a graduate of Eaton and Oxford. Following the Revolutionary War, he became governor general of Canada, during which time the Duke of Rochefoucault-Liancourt described him as having an "inveterate hatred against the United States." Simcoe described his old foes as a "mean and despicable enemy." (David Memorial Library.)

This re-enactor is dressed in the uniform of the Queen's Rangers. The Queen's Rangers were cavalry men recruited from American loyalists. Their green uniforms were so similar to those worn by Lee's Lighthorse Brigade that, during the raid, Simcoe was able to impersonate Lee's quartermaster and draw forage from an American depot. (Brigade of the American Revolution.)

Following the destruction of the troop boats at Finderne, Simcoe began his return to Staten Island. The road led to Somerset Court House (Millstone). From there, he planned to take Amwell Road through Franklin and turn right at Garret Voorhees's house. By that time, he hoped he would be pursued by the New Jersey militia. He had set an ambush at South River with a contingent of British Infantry commanded by Major Richard Armstrong. (H. (Hap) Heins Collection.)

Upon reaching Somerset Court House, Simcoe found three loyalists were being held prisoner in the courthouse and jail. He released the prisoners and burned the courthouse. The flames ignited two nearby houses. Following the war, the county seat was moved to Somerville, where a new courthouse and jail was built on land donated by Cornelius Tunnison next to his tavern (see p. 102). (Davis Gray Collection.)

Because the British had burned the Garret Voorhees House in June 1777, Simcoe failed to turn toward the ambush he had set for his pursuers at South River. Instead, he continued down Amwell Road, unaware that he had been recognized when he stopped at the Frelinghuysen Tavern in Bound Brook, and that an ambush had been set for him on the outskirts of New Brunswick. There, Captain Moses Guest (right) and 35 militia men captured Simcoe. He was secretly held prisoner in the Barnardus LaGrange House in New Brunswick to prevent him from being lynched by the outraged citizenry (see p. 21). (Rutgers Special New Jersey Collection.)

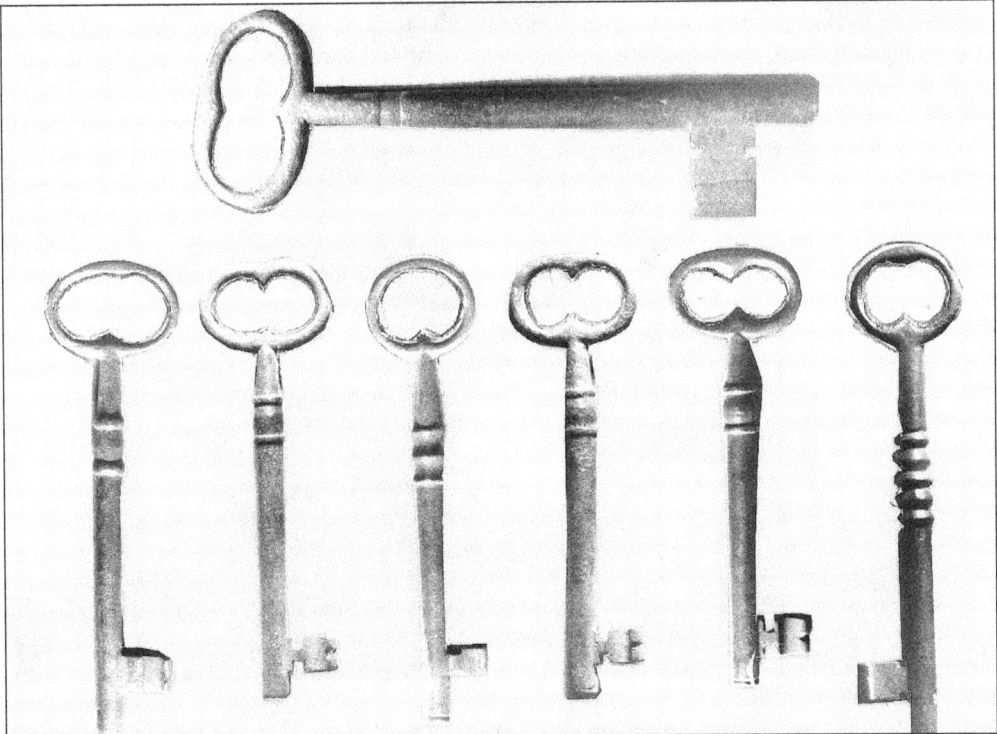

These keys are all that is left of the Somerset County Court House, which was burned by the Queen's Rangers on October 26, 1779. The top key fits the front door. The other keys are for the meeting rooms and jail cells. (Swan Historical Foundation.)

Other sites of interest in Millstone include the Old Millstone Forge, shown above. The forge was in continuous operation from 1693 until 1959, when the last blacksmith, Edward Wyckoff, died at the age of 88. Wyckoff had worked in the forge since the age of 10. During that time he shod an average of nearly 30 horses a month. The forge is open to the public and has an interesting collection of antique tools. (Somerset County Historical Society.)

During the British and Hessian occupation of New Brunswick, Queen's College (now Rutgers) was moved to Somerset County for safety. Classes were held in the Peter Dumont House in Branchburg, and here, in the Van Harlingen House in Millstone. The students served as minutemen in the militia. This photograph was taken in 1905. (Rutgers Special New Jersey Collection.)

Four

FROM 1780 TO THE
BIRTH OF A NEW NATION

The army spends the coldest winter of the war at Jockey Hollow. American and French armies march south to Yorktown. The Washingtons take up residence at Rockingham during the signing of the treaty of peace. The "Father of his Country" again passes through the county on the way to his inauguration in 1789.

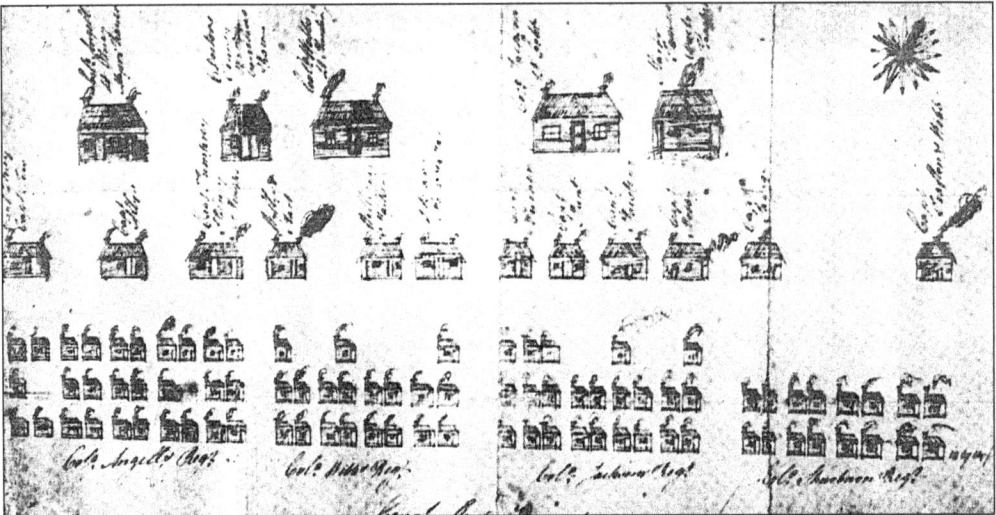

Ten thousand officers and servicemen with the Continental Line from Connecticut, Maryland, Massachusetts, New Jersey, New York, Pennsylvania, and even Canada, took up quarters at Jockey Hollow during the winter of 1779–80. Elements of the American army began to arrive at Jockey Hollow in November 1779. Each brigade was assigned a campsite. This diagram by Robert Erskine shows the hutting arrangement of General Stark's brigade. The New Jersey Brigade was camped in northern Bernardsville in Somerset County. (Erskine Hewett Collection.)

The men lived in tents while they built log cabins for the winter. Six hundred acres of oak, walnut, and chestnut trees were cut down to build rows of soldier huts such as these. General Washington was greeted with a severe hail and snow storm when he arrived on December 1. By the 14 of December, there was 2 feet of snow on the ground. (Wayne Daniels Collection.)

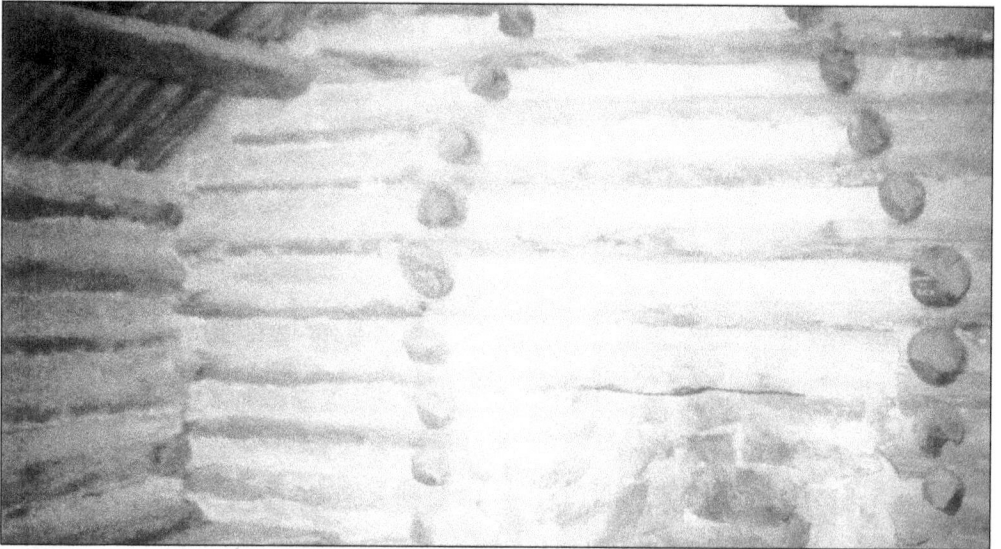

This is the inside of one of the soldier huts. Each cabin could quarter 10 to 12 men. The winter of 1779–80 was the worst on record, including that of Valley Forge; there were 28 blizzards. The Hudson River, the Raritan River, Long Island Sound, and New York Bay froze over. Teams of horses hauled wagons back and forth over the ice. Two hundred mounted British cavalrymen were able to cross from New York to Staten Island. In January, the Somerset Militia were called upon to help dig out Washington's starving army. Today, Jockey Hollow is a National Park that is open to the public. (Wayne Daniels Collection.)

Dr. John Cochran was appointed surgeon general of the middle department by General Washington in the spring of 1777. In October 1781, he was appointed director general of the Hospitals of the United States. He was, for a time, quartered with Michael Field, a miller from Bound Brook. Before there was such a thing as a vaccination, Cochran was an advocate for the far-riskier procedure of inoculation for small pox. One method of inoculation was to pass a needle and thread, dipped in puss from a smallpox lesion, under a person's skin. Almost always fatal, smallpox overwhelms the body through the respiratory system. Introducing it to a small area by inoculation, however, permitted the body to fight it off and develop immunity. (Harry Kels Swan Collection.)

Smallpox could decimate an army. General Washington decided, for the first time in history, to inoculate his entire army against the disease. The decision was kept secret so the British wouldn't learn of the American tactic, and wouldn't take advantage of the large numbers of men incapacitated with symptoms of the disease during the inoculation period. In field hospitals like this one, in Basking Ridge, Bound Brook, Hillsborough, and elsewhere, Dr. Cochran conducted the inoculations and kept the men until they recovered. (Wayne Daniels Collection.)

Nearby, in Basking Ridge, stands the largest tree in New Jersey. The 600-year-old white oak in the cemetery of the Presbyterian church stands 93 feet high with a 138-foot spread. Its trunk is 18 feet in circumference. Beneath these branches, George Whitfield preached to a crowd of 4,000 during the Great Awakening in 1740. Washington and Lafayette picnicked here, and colonial troops rested under its shade. Thirty-five veterans of the American Revolution are at rest in the cemetery. (Author's Collection.)

The John Parker Tavern, or Vealtown Tavern, in Bernardsville was built c. 1740. The tavern keeper at the time of the Revolution was John Parker, a captain in the 1st Battalion of the Somerset County Militia. During the Jockey Hollow encampments, it was a favorite place for Continental troops, including General "Mad" Anthony Wayne. Old Army Road began as a trail beaten through the forest by soldiers going from Jockey Hollow to the Parker Tavern. The ghost of Parker's daughter Phyllis is said to still search here for her lover, who was hanged as a British spy. (Author's Collection.)

This grain barn was built in 1768 to store grain for the Van Dorn mill. During the Jockey Hollow encampments, it stored grain and flour for Washington's army. Located along Route 202, north of Bernardsville, it was moved across the street and converted into a restaurant by famed restaurateur William Childs in 1930. Today it is still serves the public as The Grain House Restaurant. (Author's Collection.)

A mill associated with the grain barn was located at this site from 1768. Grain was ground into flour in the mill for Washington's army, which was encamped nearby at Jockey Hollow. The present mill, shown in this 1930s photo, was built in 1843 on the site of the original colonial mill. (Historic American Buildings Series, New Jersey #667, Library of Congress.)

This is a portrait of Marie Joseph Paul Yves Roch Gilbert du Motier, the Marquis de La Fayette, taken from a 1777 French print. Lafayette was given a commission as major general by Congress that year, but Washington refused to permit him command of American troops until he had personally raised Lafayette to the level of a third degree mason. Lafayette was wounded at Brandywine and distinguished himself as a division commander at the Battle of Monmouth. (*Lossing's Pictorial Field Book of the Revolution.*)

In February 1781, General Washington assigned Lafayette three battalions of the Continental Line, numbering about 1,200 men, with orders to march to Virginia, capture (if possible) the traitor Benedict Arnold, who was leading British forces there, and take command of the Virginia theater of operations. Foreshadowing the march of Rochambeau and the French army in 1782, Lafayette passed down the road from Morristown to Princeton, camping two nights in Somerset County. (Brigade of the American Revolution,)

Lieutenant General Jean Baptiste Donatien de Vimeur, the Count de Rochambeau (left), was sent in command of the French army to support the American Revolution in 1780. His second in command, the Duke de Lauzun-Biron (right), was a nobleman of great wealth. He was known for his engaging personality, bravery, and wit. Both men gained an appreciation for democracy and favored the French Revolution a decade later, but neither could escape their noble birth. De Lauzun was guillotined at Paris during the Reign of Terror, and Rochambeau narrowly escaped the same fate. (*Lossing's Pictorial Field Book of the Revolution.*)

Adam Philipe, the Count de Custine (left), commanded a regiment under Rochambeau and served with distinction. During the French Revolution, he joined the revolutionary party and commanded the French Army of the Rhine. During the Reign of Terror, he was recalled to Paris because he was a nobleman, and guillotined on August 27, 1793. Count Jean Axel de Fersen (right) was a Swede who had been sent to America with Rochambeau because he had become too close with Marie Antoinette while serving in the palace guard. During the French Revolution, he drove the coach carrying King Louis XVI and Queen Marie Antoinette in their failed attempt to escape from Paris. In 1810, de Fersen was murdered by a mob in Stockholm that suspected him of complicity in the death of King Christian Augustus. (*Lossing's Pictorial Field Book of the Revolution.*)

31.ᵉᵐᵉ Camp à *Sommerset* Court House les 8 Septembre 14 Miles
de Prince Town.

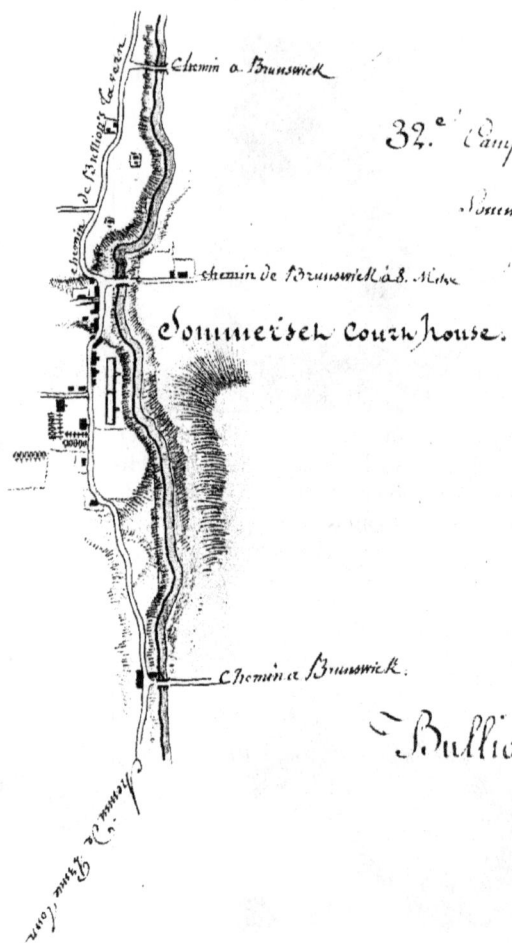

Chemin a Brunswick

32.ᵉ Camp à *Bullion's Tavern* le 9 Septembre 13 miles

Sommerset Court house.

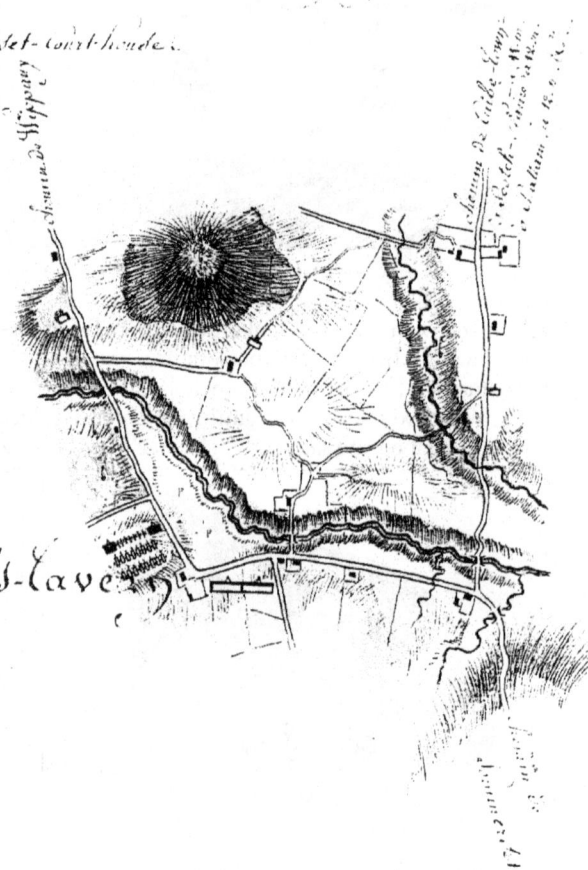

chemin de Brunswick à S. Mike

Sommerset Court House.

Chemin a Brunswick

Bullion's Cave

In August 1781, two divisions of the French army under Rochambeau passed through Somerset County, camping at Bullion's Tavern (Liberty Corner) and Somerset Court House (Millstone) on their way to the Battle of Yorktown. In September 1782, they marched north, camping in different parts of the same two towns. Rochambeau's mapmaker, Louis Alexandre Berthier, drew maps of the roads they traveled and their nightly camp sites. Here are Berthier's drawings of the two Somerset County camp sites for the return trip. (Princeton University.)

Somerset County residents lined the route of march to see the legions of King Louis XVI pass by. The well paid and equipped French army made a magnificent impression, in marked contrast to the poorly clad Continentals. Here are two of the many banners that flew over the French regiments. (Wayne Daniels Collection.)

Many of the French regiments wore white uniforms, which were distinguished from each other by different color facings. The Royal Deux-Ponts and the Saintonge were faced with green and the Soissonais with pink (left). The uniforms of the Auxerrois Regiment are shown on the right. (David Memorial Library.)

Nearby, in Warren Township, is the Kirsch-Ford House. Constructed in the early 1700s, it was owned by Captain Ford at the time of the Revolution, and is shown on Washington's maps. The house has been restored and is open to the public. (George Bebbington Collection.)

The King George Inn in Mt. Bethel is one of the oldest buildings in the county. The original part of the structure was constructed in 1692 as a blacksmith shop. Since before the Revolution, it has been operated as a taproom, tavern, stagecoach stop, and restaurant. (Somerset County Historical Society.)

The home at the bottom of this page was built near Liberty Corner by James and Abigail Compton between 1760 and 1770. The property contained a little over 183 acres. In a small family graveyard are the tombstones of various members of the Compton family, including James, who was a Revolutionary War soldier, and his wife, Abigail. (Historic American Buildings Survey, New Jersey #185, Library of Congress.)

Sacred
To the memory of
James Compton
who died July 28
1813 aged 62 years
7 mons & 13 days

How doth the mourning widows heart
With unknown anguish swell
And his children feel the smart
Which none can fully tell

When a band of Hessian soldiers raided the house, the young daughter, Sarah, announced that her father had gone to fight the British. While the soldiers looted the house, Sarah's mother, Abigail, sat on a chest containing the family valuables. Refusing to open it, only the intervention of one of the officers kept her from being bayoneted. Three days later, she gave birth to twins. (Historic American Buildings Survey, New Jersey #185, Library of Congress.)

This portrait, entitled *General Washington*, was painted by John Trumbull, son of the governor of Connecticut and one of Washington's aides-de-camp. Following the victory at Yorktown, the hostilities ceased, but the war continued for Britain in the European theater. The British army remained in occupation of the City of New York for the next two years. In order to preserve his victory, Washington had to keep his army intact until the treaty of peace was signed and the British army removed. (David Memorial Library.)

In August 1783, Congress convened in Nassau Hall at the College of New Jersey (Princeton) to await the signing of the treaty of peace. Washington was invited to attend the sessions, but when he arrived with Martha on August 23, 1783, there was no available lodging in the village of Princeton. Congress rented the John Berrien estate in Rocky Hill, known as Rockingham, for Washington's use. The house is shown here about 1900. (Somerset County Historical Society.)

Rockingham had more than 20 rooms. It was large enough to house the general, his wife, staff, and baggage. Washington used the "blue room" on the second floor as his study and two small adjoining rooms as his bedroom and dressing room. This is a view of the dining room. Washington had a marquee (a large tent) erected on the lawn for occasions when the number of dinner guests exceeded the capacity of the dining room. (Historic American Buildings Survey, New Jersey #18, Library of Congress.)

Three hundred troops from Maine camped around the house, awaiting their discharges, longing for home. To pass the time, they drew pictures of ships on the siding of the south side. In the blue room, Washington wrote his famous "Farewell Address to the Armies." Washington's portrait was painted here by William Dunlap, Joseph Wright, and Charles Wilson Peale. (Somerset County Historical Society.)

While at Rockingham, the Washingtons entertained many notable guests, including Robert Morris (top left), Thomas Jefferson (top right), James Madison (bottom left), and Thomas Paine (bottom right). The portraits of Morris and Jefferson are by Charles Wilson Peale and hang at Independence National Historic Park. The James Madison picture is from a 1783 miniature by Charles Wilson Peale that is housed in the Library of Congress, and the Thomas Paine picture is from an engraving by W. Sharp in the collection of the New York Historical Society.

John Paul Jones was also a guest of General Washington at Rockingham. Other guests not shown included Elias Boudinot, Oliver Ellsworth, Richard Stockton, and John Witherspoon. (Independence National Historic Park.)

Early in October 1783, Martha Washington left Rockingham to return to Mount Vernon. General Washington accompanied her as far as Trenton, where he met General Greene. The two generals rode back to Princeton together. It was the last time they saw each other. Washington remained at Rockingham until November 10, 1783. (Rutgers Special New Jersey Collection.)

With the war over, Washington returned to his plantation, Mount Vernon. He did not seek public office in the Confederation, or in Virginia. In 1787, he was requested to attend, and then to preside over, a constitutional convention in Philadelphia to revise the Articles of Confederation. Rather than revise the Articles of Confederation, that convention produced the Constitution, which, upon ratification, gave birth to the United States of America. Washington again retired to private life. The Constitution went into effect on June 21, 1788. In September, the outgoing Confederation authorized the states to select electors to elect a president of the new government. In February 1789, the electors met and sent sealed ballots to New York to be opened by the Senate. The Senate did not reach a quorum until April 6, at which time the ballots were opened, revealing that George Washington had been unanimously elected president. Word was sent to Washington in Virginia. Washington left Mount Vernon on April 16, 1789, to begin the eight-day trip to New York for his inauguration. Along the way, his route was lined with throngs of well-wishers and marked by festive celebrations. On April 22, 1789, Washington had breakfast with the president and faculty of Princeton College. He then traveled what is today Route 27, to New Brunswick. Along the way, the citizens of Somerset and Middlesex Counties turned out to raise their hats and salute the "Father of his Country" as he passed by. Washington was inaugurated in New York on April 30, 1789. (New York Historical Society.)